EVERYDAY CONFIDENCE

Boost your self-worth and build unshakeable confidence

Books by the Speakmans

Conquering Anxiety

Winning at Weight Loss

NIK & EVA SPEAKMAN

EVERYDAY CONFIDENCE

Boost your self-worth and build unshakeable confidence

First published in Great Britain in 2021 by Orion Spring
an imprint of The Orion Publishing Group Ltd
Carmelite House, 50 Victoria Embankment
London EC4Y 0DZ

An Hachette UK Company

1 3 5 7 9 10 8 6 4 2

A CIP catalogue record for this book is available from the British Library.

ISBN (Trade Paperback) 978 1 8418 8325 0
ISBN (eBook) 978 1 8418 8326 7

Printed and bound in Great Britain by Clays Ltd, Elcograf, S.p.A

MIX
Paper from
responsible sources
FSC® C104740

www.orionbooks.co.uk

ORION
SPRING

Important Information Before Reading this Book

This book is not a substitute for medical or psychological intervention, nor is the content intended to replace therapy, or medical help and advice.

While we are confident that this book will help to positively alter your perspective and attitude in relation to your confidence and yourself, there are no guarantees.

If you feel that your lack of confidence is detrimentally affecting your mental health, or is contributing to your anxiety or psychological wellbeing, we would recommend speaking to your GP.

We would also always strongly encourage you to speak with your doctor or health professional about how you are feeling, and also to enquire about therapy should you feel that this is necessary or that you need emotional help and support.

Contents

Introduction

I am inspired beyond belief . . . I totally believe you've changed my life in every aspect . . . I'm holding my head higher.

Emma

Most people know that in order to achieve good physical health you should eat well, obtain good-quality sleep and participate in exercise. However, you may not appreciate that the same rules apply for maintaining good mental health, and a significant contributor to your good mental health is confidence.

Something that you may never have considered is that no one is born with or without confidence. You are a wonderfully unique human being that has been influenced by your environment, your life and your upbringing, determining everything from your views on the world to the football team you support, the political party you prefer and even your favourite foods. This is also true of your confidence.

The truth is that it is highly likely that you have never actually had an impartial view of yourself. Your view of yourself, your capabilities, your ease to speak out or to speak in public is often based upon how others have made you feel, and the people you have encountered and interacted with throughout your life. Through these circumstances, and the words you (and others) use to describe yourself and your capabilities, your levels of confidence and self-esteem are created. These words you use and believe about your abilities are also the basis of the internal dialogue that you have with yourself.

> 'If you hear a voice within you say, "You cannot paint," then by all means paint, and that voice will be silenced.'
>
> **Vincent van Gogh**

Lack of Confidence Is a Symptom

You may feel that a lack of confidence is the problem you suffer from, and that if you could solve it, all would be well. But in truth, a lack of confidence, and all its associated emotions such as self-doubt, self-loathing, frustration, anxiety, feeling weak, feeling judged and not good enough, are symptoms of something else that needs addressing.

From working with many thousands of clients over the last two decades, we understand that a cause or causes always exist in creating your feelings of low confidence.

You were not born lacking confidence, and nor does living with a lack of confidence have to be your destiny.

We hope that reading this book will help you to locate, challenge and address the cause or causes of your negative behavioural references (known as schemas) that cause you to think and feel as you do. We want to help you not only address, challenge and positively condition these negative behavioural references that are the 'cause' of your lack of confidence, but also learn exercises that will build and increase your confidence.

Just like when you physically exercise to improve your strength, stamina and muscle definition, these mental exercises will allow you to develop and boost your confidence.

Symptom and Cause

Forever grateful to the both of you for helping me on my journey. You're incredible. Thank you for everything.
Hazel

In the 1970s there was a period in the United Kingdom when the bin collection department was on strike for a significant period of time. As a consequence, festering rubbish accumulated and bags full of waste were piled high along the roads and streets.

Inevitably, thanks to the ever-growing mounds of trash, an infestation of rats and insects ensued. Councils tried to rectify the situation by spraying insect killer and putting down rat poison. However, as one wave of insects and rats were eradicated, another wave would appear. This cycle of events carried on for some time, as the mounds of rotten trash were a symptom of the strike and similarly the insects and the rats were a symptom of the trash. It was only when the strike was over and the trash was removed that the insect and rat infestation disappeared permanently.

This is a great example of how a cause – the strike – resulted in a build-up of trash, which, in turn, caused an infestation of rats and insects. Without the trash there would have been no infestation. The same is true of behaviours: once you identify, address and resolve the cause that drives the behaviour, the symptoms will disappear almost effortlessly.

This is the basis of our approach to confidence and how we hope to help you. Our intention is to help direct you to recognise what beliefs no longer serve you, and how to remove them to give you a fresh, untarnished, uncluttered and clean foundation of confidence and self-belief.

What Is a Schema?

If you are familiar with our work, you may have heard us refer to schemas before. In simple terms, a schema is a learning we have acquired in our life. If we have been fortunate and had a positive upbringing and positive life, we will have an abundance of positive schemas that support and uplift us. Conversely, if we have endured negative life events, negative people and a negative developmental environment, then we will have a plentiful supply of negative behavioural schemas that challenge and destabilise us.

A schema is a term used in psychology, defined as: **'a cognitive framework or concept that helps organise and interpret information. Schemas allow us to take shortcuts in interpreting the vast amount of information that is available in our environment.'**[1]

Negative schemas are the culprits that cause all negative emotions and feelings, including low confidence, low self-esteem, anxiety and anxiety disorders.

Schemas, positive and negative, are the basis of all opinions, thoughts and beliefs, including our opinions, thoughts and beliefs about ourselves. The age we were when we created a schema dictates how accurate that schema is – would you trust a four-year-old's interpretation of a complex event? Yet in some ways your confidence may be unconsciously influenced by a schema established at that age. Many schemas that shape our daily actions are confused and inaccurate.

> *We continue to believe anything that we don't challenge.*

Although most childhood schemas are naturally reconditioned with new evidence as we grow and mature, some remain unchallenged. We therefore continue to use a behavioural reference or schema based entirely upon a child's perspective. This is why many of us may be self-deprecating, while family, loved ones and friends see us in an entirely different – and significantly more positive – way than we do ourselves.

Childhood schemas often inhibit elements of your life, which can then often lead to feelings of frustration and confusion as they create a conflict in how you *want* to think, feel and behave, versus how you actually *do* think, feel and behave.

The great news is that negative schemas can be changed and upgraded by challenging them positively. All schemas are learned, and this means you can learn new, more positive ones. This is the basis of our therapy and, as you read through this book, we very much hope that you will begin to see your past negative schemas, and consequently yourself and your abilities, from a far more positive perspective, thereby building on your confidence and self-worth.

> *Our thoughts create our feelings. Better thoughts create better feelings.*

Elements of Confidence

Let us remind you again that we are not born with or without confidence. Confidence is a feeling we obtain from . . .

Life experiences:

* I know I can because I have always been encouraged.
* I know I can because I have been taught to believe in myself.
* I know I can because I have never felt judged negatively.
* I know I can because I have been taught to be confident.
* I know I can because I have been taught that the very worst that could happen is that I will learn from my mistakes.
* I know I can because I have been taught to make light of my mistakes.

Practice:

* I know I can because I have done this before.
* I know I can because I have perfected it.
* I know I can because this is my skill.
* I know I can because I do this all the time.

Deserving:

* I deserve praise for my skills.
* I deserve to be appreciated.
* I deserve to be happy.
* I deserve to stand out.
* I deserve to be outstanding.

This means that you don't have to feel confident to learn confidence. It is not something that you're either born with or without. Our intention through this book is to show you that confidence is something you can develop and grow through your life experiences, through practice and through learning that you deserve to feel your confident best every day.

Everyday Confidence

Even those who believe they have no confidence, are confident at something and this alone is something to be proud of.

It is natural for our confidence to rise and fall as a consequence of external life experiences. For example, your confidence can soar when you get a new job or are given a sincere compliment, yet it can plummet in a moment when something goes wrong or someone says something hurtful. The trick is to find a way to maintain your inner confidence regardless of what is happening in your life. A foundation of inner confidence will give you a sense of self-belief and self-trust even when things are difficult, as they are for everyone sometimes.

Be assured that you are not alone if you feel lacking in confidence. So many people we meet and speak to appear outwardly confident, yet the truth is that they feel fragile and terrified on the inside. Many are fearful of being discovered as a fraud, as the reality is that they feel they do not possess a single ounce of confidence.

While you may not see this now, while you may feel alone in your worries, as you read through this book and relate to some of the real-life case studies that we share, you will encounter many others who have been where you are and have learned to become more confident. These realisations will help you to cultivate your confidence and, even more, your self-esteem. Cultivating confidence will not only help you to feel better, more successful and more confident; it will encourage your better physical health, and also aid positive mental health, too.

As your confidence grows with practice and as you alter past negative schemas, you will begin to feel worthy of good health, true happiness and achieving goals you had only previously dreamed of.

Having confidence will encourage others to believe in you, too, and will allow you to attract success as you begin to feel capable of stepping out of your comfort zone, connecting with yourself and others.

In this book we want to help you build, develop and appreciate your true self-worth and value, so as to give you inner and unstoppable everyday confidence.

We believe in you. We are humbled that you have picked up our book, and we hope that you will accept and embrace the information and exercises within and that you will enjoy your journey to greater confidence.

1

Our Therapy

I was possibly one of the most anxious, depressed, self-loathing people you could possibly meet. I booked a place on your Upgrade Your Life workshop and I was TERRIFIED.

Then something happened to me that literally changed everything! I was chosen to participate in Nik and Eva's Mirror Technique exercise [see page 220]. Looking at myself and describing what I saw, all I heard from my mouth were things I would never think about anyone else, let alone say out loud. With the rest of the technique working on seeing myself in that mirror more positively, my life finally began with many tears of relief but also happiness.

Since then I have become the mum and wife I always wanted to be. I am no longer scared to go out and have gone back to work full time in an extremely fast-paced role, which I love and am good at.

Best of all . . . I am ME, and I like me.

Emma P.

Our Schema Conditioning Therapy for Confidence

This book is about helping you. We really want you to have the closest experience possible to having a session with us in person, and therefore we would like to start our journey together by explaining to you the basis of our therapy in a way that is personal to you, which you can identify with. Once you understand our method, you can relax and know that we will share information and suggestions with you, to help you see yourself from a different, more positive perspective. Once you accept and adopt this new perspective on your past life events, you can begin to lay the foundations for building a more positive attitude towards yourself. You can start to get to know and cultivate the person you truly are and aspire to be. It is likely that you have never yet been acquainted with the confident, vibrant person you really are, and we sincerely hope that our book will provide you with that opportunity.

> *Your opinion of yourself is often based upon how other people have made you feel.*

With that in mind, we would like you to consider the following scenario: a good friend, Charlie, asks you to join him on a night out with some of his work colleagues, who you have never met. Despite you being apprehensive, Charlie convinces you to come and promises that his group of work colleagues are lovely and great fun. However, Charlie then goes on to give you a little advice about a new member of the group, Mary. Charlie warns you to keep your distance from Mary, as once she starts a conversation with you, she talks only about herself and is rather monotonous and difficult to escape from.

You go on the night out and do your utmost to avoid Mary, as you already have an opinion of her (a schema), based upon what Charlie has told you. In essence, Charlie has influenced and taught you how to perceive Mary. As the evening progresses, you spot Mary speaking to members of the group and pity the poor person that Mary has targeted, yet you yourself have not yet spoken with her. However, while sat momentarily on your own, Mary returns from a visit to the bar and you suddenly find yourself cornered as she sits herself next to you. You feel a sinking sensation in your chest but, being polite, you respond to Mary's introduction and cautiously engage in pleasantries with her. Before you know it, you find yourself in an engaging, interesting and enjoyable conversation with her.

Your previous opinion of Mary is soon forgotten as you happily chat away, even exchanging friend requests on Facebook. As you leave at the end of the evening, and thank your friend for inviting you, you both reflect on the night out. In that moment you realise that the person you most enjoyed speaking to was Mary. When you question Charlie's advice about Mary, and share your positive experience, you are surprised that your friend replies, 'To be fair, I've never really given her the time of day as it was another colleague who pre-warned me about her.' After a little thought Charlie adds, 'But in hindsight, that colleague is rather negative and doesn't have a good word to say about anyone.'

In that moment, both your and Charlie's opinion of Mary is immediately positively conditioned, and any apprehension about being her friend in the future immediately disappears. You both realise that you misunderstood the situation and unfairly judged Mary.

With this new evidence that you have obtained, both your and Charlie's schema about Mary changes instantly and indefinitely. You don't ever have to remind yourself that Mary is a nice lady, and you don't have to go home and work on changing your opinion of her because the inaccurate schema you had has now been positively conditioned with the overwhelmingly positive evidence you collected.

This metaphor is a great example of how our therapy works and how you yourself can change, without needing multiple meetings with us for you to keep asking why you should no longer think Mary is a boring, unpleasant person or for us to remind you that Mary is actually nice.

Once your belief has changed, it totally changes how you feel, forever.

If you are reading this book because you have low confidence, the likelihood is that you also have a number of negative schemas about yourself and your abilities. Many of these, like the advice given by your friend Charlie in the example on the previous page, are untrue and inaccurate. We want to help you unmask the origins of those limiting negative schemas, and to provide you with the opportunity to challenge them and positively condition your beliefs about yourself.

In the example above you were led to believe something that was untrue about Mary. Just as you were given the opportunity to meet Mary for yourself and form your own opinion of her, our hope is that reading this book will allow you to meet the true person that you really are, without the actions or opinions imposed upon you by others. Knowing your true self will allow you to emerge from underneath the shadow of those negative and inaccurate schemas and see yourself without judgement and with the clarity to recognise the incredible human being you really are.

Our Questionnaire

So, let's get started. Welcome to your first session with us.

We all have life events that can cause a lack of confidence, a lack of self-esteem, a fear of being judged and a lack of self-belief. Many of us will not even realise what these life events were, or how they affected us, so let us find out more about you. We would like to help you discover what events may have created negative schemas that today contribute to your lack of confidence. Let us help you look for clues. We will also be asking you to consider the positive elements of your life, too, which we will ask you to consider once more when you have finished the book. The reason for this is that you should see more positive and happy memories begin to surface once they are released from the weight of negative past events.

Grab a pen and paper, and write down your answers to the following questions:

* **Briefly describe your typical day. Describe what you do and the people you surround yourself with (they will often impact how you feel, so it is very important to consider this).**

* **What events, people or experiences have contributed to making you the way you are? Please be specific and list both:**
  1 Positive events, people and experiences.
  2 Negative events, people and experiences.
  As you read through the book, these are potentially the negative schemas you will need to address, challenge and condition with contrary evidence.
  When you think of each negative experience, score the negative feeling it brings up in you out of ten – ten being the worst, zero being no negative feeling at all. When you have finished the book, go through these negative events and score each one again to highlight what has changed and what still needs to be worked on.

* **What would you say are your biggest personal:**
  1 Successes?
  2 Regrets?
  3 Failures? When you have finished the book, note how each failure resulted in a positive lesson.

* What is your specific reason for reading this book? Noting and rereading this every time you pick up the book will help you to look for a solution to this specific problem.

* When do you believe this issue started? Knowing this will give you clues as to the time in your life when something may have occurred to create your low-confidence-causing schema.

* What dreams and ambitions did you have when you were younger?

* What dreams and ambitions do you have now? This will help you to reflect on the things from childhood you may still like to work towards as an adult.

* List everything in your life that you appreciate.

* List the values and qualities you appreciate about yourself.

* Score your life as you see it out of ten. Please reflect on this again when you have read the book and consider what else must happen and what actions you can take to make this score either a nine or ten out of ten.

* Score your level of confidence out of ten generally. Reflect on this periodically while reading this book, and as you practise the exercises suggested.

* In what areas of your life do you lack confidence? List them all. Examples to consider would include speaking up for yourself, speaking up for someone else you feel is

being treated unfairly, public speaking, interacting with people generally, saying what you really mean, speaking with a potential partner, dating, making new friends, asking for something for yourself such as a promotion or a better seat in a restaurant, etc., speaking to people in authority such as your boss, a doctor or a police officer, asking for a refund in a store, questioning the price of something, telling someone how you feel, telling your partner, family or friends that you love them. This question will give you clues as to the origins of where you learned to lack confidence.

* If you could attempt any one thing and you knew that you couldn't fail, what would it be?

* Finish the sentences below, writing the first thing that comes to mind:

  'Life is a ....'

  'People are ....'

  'I am ....'

  'I need ....'

  'I wish ....'

  'If only ....'

* What is your most frequent recurring thought? This will give you an idea of what occupies your mind.

* List your top ten personal successes (e.g. passing your driving test, earning a degree, getting married, getting a job, organising a party, making someone laugh, creating something, an act of kindness, speaking out about something important).

* List people you can recall meeting or have ever known who have been unkind to you. This would include people who may have said just one cutting remark or people who you barely know or are no longer in your life but you recall them due to the way they spoke to you or treated you.

* What comedians/actors make you laugh? You can't always control external events or how others may make you feel, but you can make time for laughter, and watching clips of these people will help lift your mood.

> To boost your self-esteem, you need to identify the negative beliefs you have about yourself, then challenge them.
>
> **NHS**[2]

Your Timeline

Another effective way to look for clues about why you lack confidence is to write a timeline of your life – essentially a list of significant events in your life, with one column describing positive events and another column describing negative events. Once you have completed this we'll show you how to take your time to look at each negative event and positively change your perspective on it, slowly and systematically. Dealing with past life events helps to lift an emotional weight that you may not even realise you are carrying. Once this weight is lifted, you will feel able to stand taller and face the world with confidence every single day.

It is equally important to be aware of all the positive things that have happened in your life, which should include your achievements, times you have laughed uncontrollably, been somewhere exciting, fallen in love, been loved by a person or pet, carried a task out confidently, said or done something that was appreciated by others, experienced an amazing date, a fantastic concert or other memorable events. Reread your positive events on your timeline regularly to remind you of the great things you have done, seen, achieved and experienced.

With the negative list, it is also important to consider events from childhood and school, when you may have been bullied, targeted or embarrassed, or there may have been an occasion when you felt you had been publicly humiliated, when someone may have said something unkind or undermined something you did. Also consider times when you may have felt belittled, chastised or mimicked. Also consider your parents, family and siblings. Did they do or say something that still hurts you today or is still vivid in your mind as an adult, despite it occurring when you were a child? Sometimes small and seemingly unimportant comments can have a big impact on us.

Were you the eldest or middle child? Consider how you felt with the arrival of a new younger sibling. Were you fostered or adopted? It is important to consider how you felt about things when they happened. As you begin to work through and challenge each negative event from your past, it is better that you focus on just one event at a time, ensuring that you read your positive list before and after.

To address each negative event, you will challenge it with positive counter-evidence, in order to alter and condition each negative schema associated with that event. This will help to reduce the negative effects of each memory. To achieve this, it is important to find something to help you feel better about each event. This may be acknowledging that you may have misunderstood (as with the example we shared about Mary). It may be that you have learned something new from what happened, or that it made you stronger, kinder, more empathetic or able to help somebody as a result of what you have been through. It may also have been just the behaviour or opinion of one person and therefore you should challenge and consider that person's intent, their experience and the possibility that their own issues caused them to behave in the way that they did. Also consider if the situation that causes you pain is something that has been and gone, and is now over. If so, you are no longer a victim of that event or person; you survived it and therefore you became a survivor, a victor. Imagine if a friend approached you who had experienced this particular life event – what would you say to them to help them feel better and more positive?

Look at each negative event on your timeline. Read what you have written and then add the words 'but luckily . . .' and then complete the sentence. For example: 'I was bullied at school, but luckily I also made some lovely friends,' or 'but luckily I survived and came away with an education'.

We have found these two small words can help you to reframe negative situations in ways that are meaningful and profound. As Tina wrote to us on Twitter:

@the_speakmans 'but luckily' . . . absolute genius – two words that have really helped me today. Thank you.

Tina

Alternatively, you can change your emotional attachment to a negative event by accepting that it was not personal to you. For example, if you have experienced an abusive relationship, you can begin to consider, and then learn to accept, that this abusive behaviour was not instigated by you, nor was it personal to you. Your abusive partner will have been abusive in the past and is likely to continue to be abusive in the future. It was the abuser who had the issue, not you. It is the abuser who should feel guilt and shame, not you. Had their actions been acceptable then they would not have hidden them or conducted them behind closed doors or away from teachers, police, your parents, etc.

> **We all do our best, until we obtain new information that allows us to do better.**

As you read through this book and the case studies we share, there may be some circumstances that are similar to yours, which will also help you challenge your own schemas. However, if, after reading this book and considering the suggestions, you are struggling to change a negative event with a more positive perspective, try speaking to a therapist or a positive friend that you trust. Explain to them that a painful memory is still affecting you today, and ask if they could offer you any suggestions to be able to see the event in a more positive light, so that you can sever that emotional tie and leave the event in the past.

When you are starting to feel better about the event, move on to the next one on your timeline, so that you can systematically work through all your painful memories to ensure they have no effect, or a lesser effect, on you today.

Be gentle with yourself as you work through your timeline. Confronting the pain of the past can be demanding, but carrying the past is an unnecessary weight on your shoulders that does not impact your life in a positive way. So even if you find it difficult to lessen the negative emotion, you can start by making a decision to remind yourself that what you endured should not have happened, that you didn't deserve for it to happen, and that it is now over.

In any event, a completed timeline is a great tool to take with you if you are having or seeking therapy, as you can direct your therapist to all the areas in your past that you would like to work on and improve. We like to remind clients at our workshops:

> *You have already survived your very worst day.*

We send timelines along with our therapy questionnaires to all our clients, and often we receive more than one page back – in fact, the record so far was one lady sending us seventy-three timeline pages, as she had so many life events to deal with. Bearing that in mind, do not worry how many pages you complete, as long as it allows you to find the answers you need.

And now it's time for your own timeline.

It is a great idea to use or create a specific notebook or computer file to store, write or document your timeline. This will enable you to work through some of the suggestions we share in a more organised way and to refer back to the timeline. It is a good way to see your journey to confidence as a project and investment in yourself. You will be working with your timeline a lot throughout this book, returning to it often and adding to it. So make sure you create it in a way that allows you to revisit and amend it easily.

We have created a very simple example of a completed timeline to give you an idea of how yours might look. Yours will have much more detail, as you'll see in the guidelines opposite.

POSITIVE	AGE	NEGATIVE
Grandad was lovely and kind but he didn't stand up to Grandma.	2	Brought up mainly by Grandma, who was strict and critical. Mum had to work.
Loved first primary school.	4	Sister was born and became the apple of my parents' eye.
	8	Had to move school because of Dad's job. Couldn't settle, had no friends, was very lonely. Grandad ill.
Family holiday to Florida.	9	
	10	Was sick in assembly. Everyone laughed. I was called names after that and laughed at. Grandad died.
	11	Mum and Dad divorced. Phobia of vomit started.
Bridesmaid at Dad's wedding.	13	Mum angry at me for getting on with Dad's new wife. She said I'm disloyal and that she was ashamed to call me her daughter. Bullying started at school. Realised best to keep my head down. Would spend a lot of time alone in library.
Did really well in my exams. Dad bought me my first designer bag.	16	No praise from Mum.
Met Ryan, my first love.	17	Met Ryan, my first love.
Good A-level grades and place at university.	18	Ryan cheated. Took him back but he kept cheating.
Passed driving test.	19	Ryan dumped me.

Met Tom at university.	20	
Started working in law firm. Still can't believe I got the job.	23	Mum said law firm was poor and not very professional. Shattered my excitement.
Married Tom.	24	Wedding was overshadowed by Mum. Said she wouldn't come if Dad's wife came. Very stressful.
Poppy born. Sister married.	26	Mum didn't visit me or come to see Poppy for over a week. Said busy with arranging sister's wedding. Didn't feel confident enough to be bridesmaid. Caused a huge argument.
Joshua born.	28	Joshua has some health issues. Lots of hospital visits. Mum said my fault as I didn't stop working.
Tom started his own company. Very proud.	29	
Road trip with Tom and children in USA. Sister has twins.	31	Mum is doting grandma to sister's children but rarely bothers with Poppy and Josh.
Tom's business expanded. More branches opened.	36	Struggle to join Tom for his business functions. Feel I'm letting Tom down but feel I'll just embarrass him.

Consider each negative event on your timeline, and whether it still affects you or causes you any discomfort or anxiety. Score the negative event out of ten (zero means it has no negative effect and ten means you feel an extreme negative reaction).

If you have scored anything in the negative life event column that is a six or above, this could very well contribute to your lack of confidence and may have created negative behavioural schemas that affect you today. Every event listed will need to be challenged in order to positively alter your perception, conditioning the schema created at that time. Once conditioned more positively, you will be able to change your resulting behaviours.

If you can see an event for what it really was and not how it felt at the time, this will allow you to become emotionally distanced from it. You can then become a third-party observer of that past life event, as opposed to allowing the memory to play in your subconscious and affect your present. You will notice, for example, that when your friends have a problem, while you may be upset for them, you have no emotionality associated to their problem because you do not have a personal attachment to the issue. Therefore you are able to soothe them and then forget what happened. This is where we want you to be when you think about your own negative memories.

You will see many examples as you read on, but to start you off right now we would like you to go through each negative event in your timeline and ask yourself the following questions, to begin to positively condition and alter the negative schemas:

* **Was it personal? For example, was someone mean to you specifically, or were they a person who was unkind to everyone? If the latter, the event was not specifically about you. Perhaps the person who made you feel bad had low self-esteem themselves, or had a difficult upbringing, so they knew no different.**

* **Might you have misunderstood the situation? If so, consider the factors that may have caused you to misunderstand, such as your age, your inexperience, feeling emotional, or not having all the facts.**

* Was the incident you experienced just an unfortunate accident?

* What did you learn from the situation? Did the event make you stronger, wiser, more compassionate to others?

* What good came from that? Did the event make you more charitable, or perhaps more understanding of others?

* Can you pity the perpetrator for having been taught to be unkind? For example, are they a bully because they themselves were bullied or because they have or had low self-esteem? Did they come from a home in which they witnessed bullying, so it was a learned behaviour as opposed to purposeful?

* What actually happened? Describe what happened as a third-party observer, factually and without emotion.

Reflection

As you reach the end of each chapter in this book, we would strongly recommend that you reflect back on your timeline, particularly the negative column, and consider:

* Does something in that chapter reflect something in your timeline?

* Has something in the chapter brought another negative life event to your mind that you had not previously added to your timeline? If so, you should add it as the memory surfaces.

The Past

None of us is immune to bad things happening, and we often get trapped in a past event without realising that we had no control over what happened to us, and forgetting that, despite everything, we survived it.

Traumatic life events can often feel so personal and make us feel worthless and weak, but please know that you are not alone. We have all had life challenges – some worse than others – but we invite you to take solace in the fact that you got through all your issues. You survived your worst ever day and you have managed to achieve numerous incredible things despite your lack of confidence.

You may not be able to forget the events that have affected your confidence, but you can certainly change your perception of them. You can cut the emotional ties and leave the events that led you to doubt yourself and therefore negatively impacted your confidence in the past. You deserve to be happy and confident. So, very well done for taking the action needed to start work on improving yourself, your self-esteem and, as a consequence, your confidence.

> **'Whether you think you can, or you think you can't – you're right.'**
> **Henry Ford**

2

The Speakmans' Schema Conditioning Psychotherapy

Our time together has changed my life. I can now visit shops with confidence and I am improving. I am very thankful. Xxx

Bev

In this chapter, we will share the method and process that we use when working with clients suffering from low confidence, in the hope that you can start to remove your barriers, dilute your fears and positively change your perspective on painful memories that hold you back. We want you to realise your potential and your positive future, free from the burdens of the past. After all, we only get one life – this is not a dress rehearsal, therefore life is for living!

We believe that deep inside, everyone knows the person they would love to be and the life they would love to live. Let us remind you that you deserve it. Yet happiness and emotional peace can often seem so unattainable, with numerous invisible barriers, negative thoughts, fear of judgement and various fears and anxieties preventing us from living that life.

How Does Our Therapy Work?

Having observed our therapy and our work – whether in person, at our workshops, on television, or via the films on our website and YouTube channel – many people comment that the solution often appears to be too simple. In fact, we hear frequently that 'Surely it can't be that easy?' The truth is that usually it is! We hope that by reading the many successful case studies within this book, you will find personal references and similarities that will enable you to address your own challenges.

You guys literally changed my life . . . Amazing, and thank you again.

Trish

As you will see from the case studies we share, we usually manage to help people significantly, or even fully, within only *one* therapy session. We have such a fast and positive impact because our clients complete a very detailed questionnaire (see page 14) prior to meeting us.

From this, we are able to understand the potential life traumas and events that may have caused our clients' anxieties, fears, insecurities, self-esteem issues and lack of confidence so that we can then prepare a personalised therapy session for them.

Conditioning Your Negative Schemas

We want to make addressing and changing your negative schemas simple. This amazing process of overcoming your confidence issues should be as straightforward as possible, so that you can get on with the important job of making yourself happier, feeling more fulfilled and allowing your life to flow more easily.

However, there is work involved on your part. Once you have our formulas, suggestions and information, we pass the baton over to you, asking you to use them to challenge your own life. Furthermore, like anything you wish to do well, there is also an element of practice. For example, when you pass your driving test you have proved yourself to be a safe and proficient driver. But for driving to become instinctive and natural, you have to practise. If you are a driver, you will recall the weeks after passing your driving test when you drove consciously and very cautiously, with full concentration. Whereas after a month or so, you can easily drive while talking to others and thinking about what to cook for dinner and where you are going as opposed to the actual mechanics of driving. The same applies with confidence, and we will share exercises to help you. Imagine a muscle. The more times you exercise it, the stronger and more pronounced it gets. We will be helping you to find and exercise your 'confidence muscle'.

Upgrading

We remember buying our first iPhones and being amazed at how they saved us so much time by allowing us to access our emails on the go. Years on, our iPhones and Android phones have become total mobile computers and are present in almost every moment of our lives. We update them regularly, making sure they are running on the latest software and functioning at their best. How amazing would it be if everyone had that same determination to upgrade their own thought processes and beliefs, and therefore subsequently updated their behaviours in line with their ever-changing lives?

Take a few moments now to consider how you see yourself. How do you perceive your confidence, your popularity, your personality and your abilities? Consider how many of these negative beliefs are stopping you from achieving the things you want, and are therefore not needed or are even unhelpful in your life. These beliefs you have will be behaviours from older operating systems and ideas you had from opinions and perceptions formed when you were younger. Just like your phone, it's time to upgrade your own operating systems – your schemas – to offer you the best possible life, free from low confidence and unnecessary anxiety.

The Speakman Way

I am shocked that you have resolved an issue that I have had for a considerable length of time. Many thanks.

Jackie

A schema allows us to organise and interpret information. It is a learned or copied pattern that becomes an automatic reference for how we think, act and ultimately behave. In our therapy, we help locate negative schemas that are a result of past negative life events. These may have evoked emotions such as shyness, embarrassment, lack of confidence, vulnerability, fear, envy, grief or shame. Once we have identified the negative schemas we help to update and mentally restructure the memory of the event, thereby amending and upgrading the negative emotions to positive ones.

The therapy that we have developed over the last two decades is called 'schema conditioning psychotherapy' (not to be confused with 'schema therapy', a different type of therapy to the one we created and not one we practise).

Schemas direct our behaviour

In 1952, psychologist Jean Piaget defined a schema as 'a cohesive, repeatable action sequence possessing component actions that are tightly interconnected and governed by a core meaning'.[3] In simple terms, schemas are the basic building blocks of intelligent behaviour and a way of organising knowledge. You could also think of schemas as files containing vast amounts of information, which are stored in the filing cabinet of your memory. Each file tells us exactly how to react when we receive incoming stimuli.

Schemas are 'learned references' that allow us to be proficient in everything we do – from brushing our teeth to driving our car; from how we communicate to how we react to seeing a spider. Our brain effectively takes a shortcut to save it having to process repeated experiences every single time. If we activate the 'brushing teeth' schema our brain saves energy by running the schema instead of reminding you of every step of the process.

Another example is having a meal in a restaurant; a schema that most of us will have developed over years of dining out. Your schema will be a pattern that includes looking at the menu, choosing your food, ordering the food, eating it and paying the bill. Whenever you are in a restaurant, you will run this same schema.

The blank canvas of new life

We are all born with a small number of innate schemas. These are the cognitive structures underlying our reflexes. For example, babies have a sucking reflex that is triggered by something touching their lips, and a grasping reflex, stimulated when something touches their hand.

But aside from these instinctive schemas, every healthy, typical brain has the same lack of knowledge at birth. As we grow up, we learn from our parents, extended family, friends, peer groups and our own individual experiences of our surroundings. Our personal processing of the world completely dictates how we see ourselves and our environment, and how we behave and react to any event or situation that we are faced with.

This means that most of our schemas are learned – as a result of copying the behaviour of our parents or people we're in close contact with, or through our own interpretation of personal life experiences.

It's important to recognise that just as behaviours can be learned, they can also be changed. We can learn a new behaviour at any time we choose.

Developing schema conditioning psychotherapy

While Nik started studying psychology at the age of twenty, Eva didn't start until we met nearly thirty years ago. Since then we have studied and trained in various fields of therapy and in doing so we identified that our skills lay in helping people change their mindsets, and subsequently their behaviours, just by talking with them and encouraging them to look at situations from a different perspective.

We believe that every individual possesses an inner wisdom. Our method is about helping people tap into their understanding of why they think and behave the way they do. Our talking therapy helps our clients reach a new understanding of the self, which can change their negative schemas. Empowering *you* to make the change is the foundation of our therapy, and why we so passionately want to share with you the secret to overcoming your lack of confidence. The good news is that the power to overcome your low confidence is already within you.

There is sometimes a misconception that our method involves some kind of magic, hypnotherapy or confusion techniques, but let us reassure you that our therapy is no more than a straight-talking conversation.

Have you ever had a lightbulb moment in a conversation with a friend, where you realised something that had previously escaped you? Something that changed the way you thought or behaved afterwards? We like to think our therapy works in the same way.

A simple change in perspective

We are all a product of our environment.

Your lack of confidence is driven by your negative schemas – but all schemas can be changed. Here's a simple example.

The British public are known for their love of talking about the weather, and a national schema is to complain about the cold and rain. However, in July 2019 the UK endured a heatwave. We experienced back-to-back days of scorching temperatures and sunshine; our lawns were brown, our plants were wilting and we suffered sticky, sleepless nights. People started complaining about the heat as it had gone on for too long. We didn't want the heatwave to last – watching the country change felt unsettling, and when it started to rain we were joyous!

Our national schema of complaining about terrible weather was transformed by the heatwave into one of complaining about endless sunshine! You could say that the schema was one of simply complaining about the weather, full stop.

Changing your mind

Another example of how schemas can instantly change and be 'conditioned' is if you learned that a friend you care about and trust has stolen from you or spoken badly about you. Receiving this new information about a trusted friend provides you with an alternative perspective, and your schema about that friend changes immediately. As a result, your behaviours and feelings towards them also change.

Essentially this is how our therapy works: we help to change your perspective forever, and it can happen immediately. Our skill, honed by many years of practice and experience, is being able to see an alternative perspective very quickly, and then effectively and precisely delivering it to the person we are helping.

The five steps of schema change

These are the five steps we use to help change schemas. Follow them to address and alter your lack of confidence, too.

1   Find the original event that knocked your confidence. Remember that you may have more than one event that has caused your lack of confidence, and that's perfectly normal. Just concentrate on one at a time from your timeline.

2   Question how you interpreted the event at the time when it occurred. How old were you, and how did you perceive the event at that age? Consider how your perception then could be flawed or inaccurate. Now try seeing it from an adult's perspective. Does your interpretation change?

3   Collate contrary evidence to positively condition your perception of the event and your resulting schema. If you find it difficult to challenge your current belief, ask a friend who you consider wise and positive. Explain that you're trying to improve your feelings by looking for a positive alternative perspective to a past negative memory.

You will also find many examples to assist you with this throughout this book.

4 See the event for what it was and not how it felt to you in the past. If this experience had happened to your friend rather than to you, how might you have seen it differently? Does the distance of imagining it happening to someone else help you to gain perspective?

5 Decide to be a victor, not a victim. If things from your past continue to affect you then you are still a victim of that person or event. Make a decision today that you will be the victor of your past: you survived everything that happened and you are prepared to positively alter your perspective to set yourself free.

> *We believe that our words and individual thoughts have a power greater than any psychiatric medicine.*

3

Confidence and Self-esteem

You have taught me how to see things in a better way . . .
You made me realise we do not have to be unhappy . . .
You provided me with tools for a future I only dreamed of.
Sharon

When looking to raise your confidence, it is vital to consider and address your self-esteem. We often use the words confidence and self-esteem interchangeably, but they are actually two quite different concepts, and it's helpful to understand that both need to be addressed when trying to attain everyday confidence.

In this chapter we will explore both concepts further, as well as helping you to understand your current levels of self-esteem and confidence. Identifying where you are now will help you to be clear about how you wish to improve, and allows you to measure your improvement throughout this journey of attaining confidence.

No one is born with or without self-esteem or confidence. Both are created as a consequence of our life experiences, the examples we are set and the people and support structures we have in place during our life, particularly in childhood and adolescence.

> *How you see yourself is based upon how other people have made you feel.*

What Is Self-esteem?

Self-esteem is the opinion we have of ourselves.

NHS[4]

Self-esteem refers to how you perceive, see and feel about yourself. Self-esteem develops from your childhood developmental years, the experiences you have had and the situations that you have been involved with which have shaped how you view yourself today.

The word 'esteem' comes from the Latin word *aestimare*, which means 'estimation, evaluation and valuation'. Your self-esteem therefore is your estimation, valuation and evaluation of yourself.

Self-esteem is our cognitive perception of ourselves. It's almost like your own personal curriculum vitae (CV) that you carry with you. You will judge from your self-created CV what you believe you can or cannot do, and also what you feel you deserve or do not deserve. Your self-esteem is the foundation of how you think, feel, decide, act and behave towards yourself and the rest of the world. It is also the description of the person you see when you look in a mirror. However, have you ever considered that who you are is based upon the words you use to describe yourself?

When you have low self-esteem you will usually see yourself, and your life, in a negative and detrimental manner, feeling inadequate and not good enough. You may find that you hide yourself away, avoiding relationships, social situations and opportunities to further your life, happiness or career.

Conversely, if you have a high level of self-esteem you are comfortable with the person you are and the decisions you make. You do not need to seek validation from third parties. People with high self-esteem are generally believed to be happier and healthier, as they are more likely to care for themselves, invest in themselves and respect themselves.

> **Self-esteem has a strong relation to happiness . . .**
> **we are persuaded that high self-esteem does lead to**
> **greater happiness.**
> **M. Rosenberg, 1965**[5]

Symptoms of Low Self-esteem

These are a few of the characteristics of an individual with low self-esteem. Perhaps some of these will resonate with you:

* **You are overly self-critical.**

* **You do not take compliments well.**

* **You assume any compliment that you are given is untrue, or just given to please from someone who is biased, such as a parent.**

* **You see yourself as less capable than others.**

* **You see yourself as less attractive than others.**

* **You rarely talk about yourself.**

* **You do not see yourself as having attained many achievements in your life.**

* **You justify your achievements as 'luck'.**

* **You do not give yourself compliments.**

* You never think you are good enough.

* You prefer to remain under the radar.

* You avoid standing out.

* You blame yourself, or assume it is your fault if anything goes wrong.

* You believe you are unlovable, those who love you must do so out of pity.

* You believe or assume people are talking about you behind your back.

* If you see people whispering or speaking privately, you assume they are talking detrimentally about you.

You may feel that lack of self-esteem is something that many people experience, and it's not a serious issue, but in our experience, it can develop into something more serious. Negative self-talk ('I'm useless', 'I always get things wrong', 'Nothing ever works out for me') and lack of self-belief can lead to depression. Low self-esteem can lead to self-medicating these low feelings with food, alcohol and/or drugs, which can become a serious problem if left unchecked.

Self-esteem Questionnaire

To establish your current level of self-esteem, we would like you to complete the self-esteem questionnaire below based upon the Rosenberg Self-esteem Scale.[6]
    Look at the statements below about yourself and indicate how strongly you agree or disagree, and score yourself on each statement accordingly.

Statements 1 to 5 will score as follows:

Strongly Disagree = 4
Disagree = 3
Agree = 2
Strongly Agree = 1

1 At times, I think I am no good at all.
Strongly Agree (1) Agree (2) Disagree (3) Strongly Disagree (4)

2 I feel I do not have much to be proud of.
Strongly Agree (1) Agree (2) Disagree (3) Strongly Disagree (4)

3 I feel useless at times.
Strongly Agree (1) Agree (2) Disagree (3) Strongly Disagree (4)

4 I wish I could have more respect for myself.
Strongly Agree (1) Agree (2) Disagree (3) Strongly Disagree (4)

5 In general, I am inclined to feel that I am a failure.
Strongly Agree (1) Agree (2) Disagree (3) Strongly Disagree (4)

Statements 6 to 10 will score as follows:

Strongly Disagree = 1
Disagree = 2
Agree = 3
Strongly Agree = 4

6 On the whole, I am satisfied with myself.
Strongly Agree (4) Agree (3) Disagree (2) Strongly Disagree (1)

7 I feel that I have a number of good qualities.
Strongly Agree (4) Agree (3) Disagree (2) Strongly Disagree (1)

8 I am able to do things as well as most other people.
Strongly Agree (4) Agree (3) Disagree (2) Strongly Disagree (1)

9   I feel that I'm a person of worth, at least on an equal plane with others.
    Strongly Agree (4) Agree (3) Disagree (2) Strongly Disagree (1)

10 I take a positive attitude towards myself.
    Strongly Agree (4) Agree (3) Disagree (2) Strongly Disagree (1)

We would now like you to calculate your total score. The higher your score, the higher your self-esteem would appear to be.

A score above twenty suggests that you have a healthy level of self-esteem. A score of twenty or below suggests that you would benefit from making a priority of building your self-esteem to give you the self-worth and value to allow yourself to shine and be confident. At the end of this chapter, we will share tips to help you to start to locate the origins of your low self-esteem, and then later in the book, we will share techniques to help improve and build on your self-esteem further.

> 'Because one believes in oneself, one doesn't try to convince others. Because one is content with oneself, one doesn't need others' approval. Because one accepts oneself, the whole world accepts him or her.'
> **Lao Tzu**

What Is Confidence?

While self-esteem is your opinion of yourself, and the person you perceive yourself to be, confidence is a skill that is built with practice. Confidence is also contextual, as you will undoubtedly be confident at some things, some of the time, even if that is merely being confident at making a cup of tea or beans on toast. It is helpful to realise that confidence can change according to the task at hand, as that helps you understand how it can be developed and applied to new tasks. It is also possible to have a high level of self-esteem, yet not be confident in performing certain tasks.

For example:

I have *high self-esteem*. I am not a confident singer, but I would be willing to try.

I have *low self-esteem*. I am not a confident singer, so I would not try.

I have *low self-confidence*. I am not a confident singer, but, as long as I could practise, I may be willing to try.

Confidence comes from the Latin word *fidere*, which means 'to trust'. Confidence is how capable you feel, and how much you trust in your abilities when performing a task, and this can understandably vary from situation to situation.

If you are self-confident then you trust in yourself, your ability and aptitude, regardless of the specific task. You will be more likely to experiment with new situations and to take on opportunities that come your way with enthusiasm. This is because your self-confidence is closely linked to your self-esteem, and, alongside confidence, these are linked in creating a solid basis for your everyday confidence.

Confidence

Self-confidence   **Self-esteem**

As you start to become confident in different areas of your life, you begin to increase your overall sense of self-esteem and self-confidence. So you can see that changes in one area of this triangle will have an impact in other areas.

> *We are stronger and smarter than we often think and believe.*

The more abundant your life is with hobbies, experiences, interactions with people, responsibilities, compliments and communication, the more confident and self-assured you will become, and the more validated you will feel as a person, which then cultivates and elevates your self-esteem and self-confidence. Working through the exercises in this book will help you elevate your self-esteem, which will build your self-confidence at the same time.

We want to help raise your self-esteem and self-confidence to encourage you to experiment with new tasks, and to recognise and celebrate your true self-worth. The more your self-esteem builds, the more confident you will be to try new tasks. The more new tasks you undertake and find yourself proficient in, the more confident you will become. This in turn will cultivate and build your self-esteem. So you see, your self-esteem will contribute to you creating more successful experiences, and these successful experiences will help create more self-esteem.

It is important to distinguish, however, between confidence and self-esteem, as someone can have self-confidence in a particular area, but yet not value themselves in any other.

Categories of Confidence

Thank you the Speakmans and team for an inspirational and wonderful day. I had no expectations but left with a positive energy to face my life enthusiastically. Incredible day. Many thanks.

Michelle

In our work as therapists, we like to categorise confidence into five easily identifiable types. You may find that you slip in and out of more than one category dependent upon the situation that you find yourself in. Which one do you currently recognise yourself in?

Our five basic confidence categories are:

1 Overconfident

Some may see someone who is overly confident as arrogant. People who are overconfident usually have very high self-esteem and are not fazed if unliked by others, as they have enough love for themselves without needing validation from outside. People who are overconfident rarely admit or take responsibility for anything they are involved in that might have gone wrong, yet will take full responsibility for everything that goes right. They will exaggerate their successes and believe they are the oracle of many areas of life. Overly confident people will be willing to try most things but may suggest adapting the task as they believe they know a better way. If you have picked up our book, you are unlikely to be in this category!

2 Confident

Confident people are composed, amiable, eager to try new things and keen to learn. People who are confident are usually self-assured, but not so that they appear arrogant. They can usually make decisions easily based on their evaluation of the situation and are at ease with most of the decisions they make. They accept themselves and who they are, and are willing to speak out comfortably and share their opinion or area of expertise with professionalism, clarity and enthusiasm. A confident person will usually hold their hands up if they have made a mistake, and are comfortable to be the centre of attention and a designated leader if required.

3 Contextually confident

A contextually confident person is someone who is confident about some things, some of the time. As the title suggests, they are confident in context. They may perhaps be confident at riding a bike, confident in their work, confident within their friendship circles and confident at specific tasks, while lacking confidence in anything they have not practised enough to have proved their capability to themselves. We believe the majority of people are contextually confident, as this is a confidence that is displayed sometimes. Even if you believe you have no confidence whatsoever, you may be confident at mowing the lawn or looking after your pet, which is confidence in context.

4 Fraudulently confident

Attending a job interview, interacting with your work colleagues, speaking with your boss or wanting to impress a potential love interest may push you into the realms of being 'fraudulently confident'. Fraudulent confidence is a protection mechanism, often used by those lacking confidence or self-esteem. The confidence fraud puts on a show to appear more confident, vivacious, experienced, intellectual, energetic or fun than they usually or really are.

We all become fraudulently confident for pockets of time to suit many circumstances, often afterwards giving a profound sigh of relief that it's over and we can now relax. People who have been fraudulently confident believe they were lucky to have got away with something rather than understanding that it was their skill and abilities that got them through a challenging situation. This is often referred to as 'imposter syndrome', where someone may be in a job they believe they obtained by luck rather than merit. If you suffer with imposter syndrome, you are likely to believe that you are not as competent or able as others may perceive you to be.

Fraudulent confidence is when we feel we are not being ourselves or that we have been given more value than we believe we are worth.

5 No confidence

People who have no confidence may find that they withdraw from all interactive and social situations. Alternatively, they may feel that they need a comfort blanket to hide behind, such as make-up, a hood or a mobile phone. People with no confidence often avoid eye contact and are oversensitive to criticism. They often look down at the ground or a phone, struggle to make decisions and try not to be seen. They give up easily and do not accept compliments. Someone with no confidence would not put themselves forward for a task voluntarily, and most often no confidence is found alongside low self-esteem.

What Are the Causes?

Low self-esteem and a lack of confidence can come from any situation in your past in which you felt negatively judged, humiliated, laughed at, embarrassed, targeted, abused, spoken down to, criticised, chastised, not good enough or emotionally or physically hurt.

Here are some examples of situations that we have come across in our many years of practice, which have caused people to lack confidence and have low self-esteem:

* Parents arguing/divorcing when child at a young age
* Being brought up in a volatile home
* Younger sibling or siblings being born
* Critical parents, grandparents, etc.
* A parent, grandparent or other influential adult favouring a sibling
* A teacher making you feel foolish
* A teacher embarrassing you in front of the class
* Making a mistake, and being laughed at and humiliated
* Losing a loved one
* Being bullied
* Being in an abusive relationship
* Having your heart broken
* Confusion over sexuality
* Parental teaching of 'be seen and not heard'
* Religious influence/teachings
* Being adopted, or being made to spend a lot of time with someone other than your parents
* Struggling academically at school
* Physical, emotional or sexual abuse
* Being negatively compared to someone else, such as a sibling, another child in school or school friend
* Social media (online bullying/unrealistic comparisons)

Physical Symptoms

Physical symptoms associated with a lack of confidence can be distressing and add to the fear of not wishing to speak out, be noticed or step out of your comfort zone. These physical symptoms can include:

* **Increased heart rate**
* **Dry mouth**
* **Shaking**
* **Shortness of breath**
* **Hyperventilating**
* **Sweaty hands**
* **Nausea**
* **Dilated pupils (making the world seem bigger and more scary)**
* **Sleep loss**
* **Headaches**
* **Feeling hot and clammy/blushing**
* **Upset stomach**

Addressing Confidence and Self-esteem

There are two key approaches to addressing your issues relating to lack of confidence and low self-esteem.

1 Locate and positively challenge the cause or causes to upgrade and condition your former schema or schemas, as found on the timeline you created earlier.

2 Practise to build your confidence.

As you read through this book, we will help guide you through a number of practical exercises to help you grow your feelings of confidence. To be able to build your confidence effectively, you must start collating evidence as to why you lack confidence and self-esteem. Understanding and dealing with the schemas that cause you to feel the way you do will help you build your new confidence on a strong foundation. It is important, therefore, not to skip any of the exercises we suggest as you approach them.

We would now like you to return to the self-esteem questionnaire earlier in this chapter (see page 46), and your responses to the statements.

* **Go through statements 1 to 10. If in numbers 1 to 5 you answered 'strongly agree' or 'agree', or in numbers 6 to 10 you answered 'strongly disagree' or 'disagree', please consider who or what may have made you feel this way.**

* **Note the experience, your age at the time of the experience, how you felt when it happened and how it makes you feel now reflecting on it. Score your negative emotion out of ten, zero being no negative emotion and ten being the highest level of negative emotion.**

* **If there was a person involved in this memory, how do you feel about them today? Again, score your negative emotion out of ten, zero being no negative emotion, ten being the highest level of negative emotion.**

* **Is this person or people still a part of your life?**

Later in the book we will share with you our Bungee Technique (see page 124) to help you create an emotional distance from anyone who has detrimentally affected your self-esteem. However, if you would like to take action immediately, you can also write a letter to the person who had a negative impact on you. This letter will never be sent, but writing a letter as if to that person to share how they made you feel gives you an opportunity to say all those unspoken words that weigh you down. Removing the negative thoughts and feelings from your mind and putting them on paper can be very empowering and helps to clear your head. Once the letter is written, you can ceremoniously post it into a shredder or tear it up and throw it away as you now take control and power over your past and past feelings.

Having considered your responses to the self-esteem questionnaire, we'd like you to now reflect on your timeline once more, adding any events or the actions of a person you may have previously omitted or forgotten.

In our clinic we use the timeline as the basis for areas that need to be worked upon and addressed. When we go through this process with clients we often hear, 'Wow, I'd forgotten all about that until now,' and this is why we would encourage you to make your timeline a dynamic document where you can keep adding events that you may have previously overlooked.

As you read through the many examples we share with you of possible causes of lack of confidence and low self-esteem, we want you to consider whether any of the examples shared apply to you.

Later we will help you address the negative events on your timeline. We know it's often hard to revisit these difficult times, but it is a crucial step to help you benefit from our approach. Push past the uncomfortable feelings so that you can grab the confidence we know you are capable of and achieve a high level of self-esteem so that you can see yourself for the truly remarkable person we know you are.

If nothing changes, nothing changes.

4

The
Inner Critic

Thank you for letting me see myself through the eyes of love. I remind myself of our time together and your mirror therapy if even a tiny amount of self-criticism surfaces.

I love myself, I respect myself and every day I am more confident. Enormous thanks.

Lisa

You may have wondered why, despite desperately wanting to do something, say something, experience something or try something new, an invisible block stands in your way and you find you simply cannot do it. Your heart races, you feel anxious, you feel hot or you just feel a sinking sensation as you hear yourself saying to yourself, thinking to yourself or feeling:

I can't . . .

I won't . . .

I don't . . .

I never will . . .

I don't deserve . . .

What's the point anyway?

This voice is your inner critic. It's that little saboteur that unconsciously presents you with a host of examples of why you are not worthy or capable. If you have low confidence and/or low self-esteem, then you feel you need to pay attention to what your inner voice is telling you, day in, day out.

New Behaviour

> 'If you do what you have always done, you will get what you have always gotten.'
>
> **Henry Ford**

When you walk over a grassy area for a period of time a clear path forms. The same is true of our behaviours. The chances are you have trodden the same path, creating and utilising the same neural pathway of self-criticism for some time. Like a muscle, the more you exercise this thought process, the more defined and pronounced it becomes. Further, your negative schemas result in you dismissing your achievements and positive attributes, and ignoring or just discounting compliments you are given.

However, the good news is that your brain is malleable, and neuroscientists have discovered that no matter what your age, you can create new neural pathways with new behaviours (even if these behaviours are initially carried out consciously as opposed to spontaneously). To start creating these new neural pathways and thus new behaviours, we want you to challenge your inner critic immediately. Firstly, consider the exact opposite of your negative statement. Better still, learn to restructure and rephrase it. Here are some examples:

Negative: I can't say no as I'll disappoint them.
Positive: I don't have to say no, I can just say, 'I can't on this occasion.'

Negative: I can't say no.
Positive: It's not a 'no', it's just a 'not right now'.

Negative: I failed.
Positive: I learned how not to do something.

Negative: I shouldn't have done that.
Positive: I'm proud of myself for having tried.

Negative: I am a fool for thinking I could do that.
Positive: I am courageous for having tried.

Negative: I am fat.
Positive: I may be overweight, but I can work on getting
   healthier.

Negative: I let everyone down.
Positive: I tried my best, and I learned from the experience.

Negative: I know I'll fail, I always do.
Positive: As a baby I fell many times when I was learning
   to walk, but I didn't give up and I made a success of it.
   I found a way then and I will now.

Negative: That compliment can't be true.
Positive: Thank you (as if I deny the compliment, I would be
   calling that person a liar and that would be rude).

Negative: I can't do that.
Positive: I will learn how to do that.

**A number of studies have shown that being happy has
been associated with a 13–26 per cent lower risk of
heart disease.**

Eric S. Kim et al., 2014[7]

Your Inner Voice

Your inner voice is an internal dialogue, which is influenced by the schemas that you have created in life. As we have established, these schemas are based on all of your life experiences to date and, more importantly, your personal interpretation of them all. Your internal dialogue also dictates your thoughts, questions, opinions, beliefs and values, as well as the questions you raise, the ideas you have and the actions you take.

> *If being self-critical hasn't improved your self-esteem and self-confidence, then maybe self-approval is worth a try.*

This inner voice can be positive, supportive and encouraging, or critical, negative and inhibiting. If we have had a positive life, with encouragement and nurturing from our earliest years, our inner voice is likely to follow suit and be encouraging due to a plentiful supply of positive schemas. If you have endured negative life events, with bullying, trauma or humiliation, then invariably, thanks to the negative schemas that have been created, your inner voice is likely to be more self-deprecating and its instruction less encouraging. However, it is important for you to realise that schemas do not always tell the truth. The accuracy of your schemas depends upon your age and circumstances when you created them. Schemas created at a young age and under traumatic circumstances are often inaccurate.

> *You will continue to believe anything that you don't challenge.*

Mind Reader

We would now like you to consider the following questions:

* Are you a mind reader?

* Do you know what people are thinking?

* Can you predict 100 per cent of the time what someone is about to say?

* Can you predict 100 per cent of the time what someone is about to do?

We assume that the answer to all these questions is likely to be no. You can neither read minds and thoughts nor predict what people are about to say or do. This would be a wonderful gift if it were ever possible by anyone, anywhere in the world. Sadly, it is not.

We suspect you may be wondering about the relevance of these questions.

Many of our clients have become so used to their inner critic that they actually believe everything that voice tells them. But we are here to remind you that no one is a mind reader. You simply cannot know for certain why someone behaves the way they do towards you. So we have to be careful of the stories our inner voice tells us when we are feeling low in confidence.

If you have low self-esteem or lack confidence, then the likelihood is that you have assumed numerous times that other people's thoughts have been detrimental about you. But you are not a mind reader, and neither is your inner critic. It helps to remind yourself of this when we find ourselves believing the stories our inner voice thinks are true.

For example:

* ***The group of girls sniggering or whispering at school.***
  Inner Critic: Those girls are being mean about me behind my back.
  Probable Reality: Did you ever consider that one of them may have just shared a big secret about a boy she had been dating?

* ***The group of people at work who were talking privately.***
  Inner Critic: My colleagues are all discussing how terrible I am at my job.
  Probable Reality: Did you consider that they may have been talking about another person in the office? Or perhaps discussing a collection for your birthday gift?

* ***When you had to do a speech at a party or gathering.***
  Inner Critic: Everyone thought I was awful, and they're all still laughing about it weeks later.
  Probable Reality: The likelihood is that most listeners were impressed that you had the guts to get up there and speak to everyone.

* ***When you were reading out in class and mispronounced a word, and the class giggled.***
  Inner Critic: Everyone thinks I'm stupid.
  Probable Reality: The whole class was grateful for a moment of positive distraction from an otherwise boring lesson.

* **When a parent left.**
  Inner Critic: If I had been more lovable, my parent would have stayed.
  Probable Reality: Have you considered that your parent was leaving your other parent, rather than you?

* **When someone said something unkind to you.**
  Inner Critic: I deserved this criticism, because I am a bad person.
  Probable Reality: It's likely this person had a terrible day and was lashing out at everyone, not just you.

* **When you were criticised by a previous partner or friend.**
  Inner Critic: I deserved to be criticised, because I am not good enough for them.
  Probable Reality: Perhaps they believed you were too good for them, so they were knocking you down to lessen the likelihood of you leaving them for someone else.

* **When you were bullied at school.**
  Inner Critic: I deserved this because I am weak and not worthy of respect.
  Probable Reality: Did you ever consider that just as you copied your parents' accents, the bully was possibly copying the behaviour of their own parents? And that they, too, could have been bullied? Or perhaps they felt worthless compared to you, and so defaulted to trying to pull you down. Or perhaps they had been bullied in the past, so their view was bully or be bullied, therefore it was self-protection.

* ***When a colleague at work was picking on you and your quality of work.***
  Inner Critic: I am being criticised because I am incompetent.
  Probable Reality: Did you ever consider that they were actually envious of you? Or that your work was better than theirs and they were scared that they would be exposed or found out for being inadequate?

These are just a handful of examples of how a negative inner voice can encourage you to misread situations. It is these inaccurate understandings that will hold you back from being the confident person that you can be.

You are not a mind reader, and it is essential that whenever you find yourself assuming that you are being judged, you remind yourself of this fact and literally say out loud, or in your head, 'I am not a mind reader.'

Fitting in is being a part of someone else's plan. Standing out means you are creating your own.

Famous Faces

'I am an optimistic, joyous person, but I'm also afraid and insecure.'

Sandra Bullock

Having no confidence and low self-esteem can feel like a lonely condition. There is a kind of circular pattern to low self-esteem, as lacking confidence means you are less likely to share your worries for fear of being negatively judged, which deprives you of the chance to understand that many other people feel the same way. Or your low self-esteem may lead you to feel undeserving of happiness, and you think that lacking in confidence is just something you have to live with because you are inadequate in some way.

We often look at others and assume that because someone can appear on television or stand on a stage in front of an audience that they must ooze confidence and self-esteem. However, we can never assume what people think or feel. We have worked with some well-known people in our time and we can assure you that even the most confident-seeming person has anxieties and insecurities.

You are not alone in lacking confidence. Many of the people you admire have shared your feelings of inadequacy and yet they have achieved great things. They did not necessarily achieve greatness because they were born with confidence. In fact, in many cases they achieved success despite lacking in confidence.

Here are a few big names to inspire you.

LADY GAGA

Hugely successful and talented singer, songwriter and actor Lady Gaga admitted to crippling insecurity when auditioning for *A Star Is Born*. Co-star Bradley Cooper wiped off her make-up in the audition, which she said left her feeling ugly. She admitted that this ended up being helpful, as it put her right where her character needed to be. Her emotional connection to that character won her the part – and many accolades. Personally, having watched *A Star Is Born*, we both commented on her natural beauty.

DEMI MOORE

Demi Moore seems like someone who has everything – beauty and a career as a leading lady in incredible films such as *Ghost* and *Indecent Proposal*. She was married to Bruce Willis for some years and has three grown-up children. Demi later married Ashton Kutcher, who was sixteen years her junior. However, she revealed in her memoir that a turbulent childhood had left her feeling, despite all of this success, that she was somehow fundamentally unlovable and unwanted.

ADELE

Adele is a household name and someone with an abundance of awards for her talents as a singer-songwriter, including an MBE. She has been called 'the voice of a generation' and yet surprisingly she still suffers from stage fright. She has said that this comes from a fear of letting her fans down when performing. It sounds as if, even though she has sold millions of albums, Adele may have a fear of being judged and a lack of confidence in her ability to satisfy her audience.

NICOLE SCHERZINGER

Most people know Nicole Scherzinger as the lead vocalist in worldwide hit group the Pussycat Dolls and as a judge on British television show *The X Factor*. Most would categorise Nicole in the 'stunningly beautiful' category, and she certainly appears to give a powerful impression of a woman who is strong, bold, assertive, confident and self-assured. However, it may be surprising to learn that Nicole has admitted to struggling with her self-worth.

As a consequence of her low self-esteem, Nicole battled with bulimia and described herself as 'miserable on the inside' despite her success and the portrayal of confidence.

As you can see from these examples, low self-esteem can literally affect anyone and everyone, and no one, regardless of success, beauty or wealth, is immune from feelings of self-doubt.

We hope these stories remind you that lacking in confidence does not make you a loser or a hopeless case, it just makes you human. And let these stories also remind you that you aren't a mind reader, and you have no idea how people are feeling on the inside.

Quietening Your Inner Critic

I wanted to thank you for giving me my life back.
I had my hair cut off today for charity, I would never have had the confidence to do anything like that before . . .
Holly

As you read through this book and start to recognise that you have been harsh and unfairly critical of yourself due to external situations and people you have encountered, we expect that your inner critic will start to become quieter. As we, together, systematically challenge your negative schemas and the life events that have impacted your confidence, we expect your inner critic to be silenced.

However, you must also consider practice, so that practice can become habit. For example, you may decide to become a vegetarian, yet when visiting your favourite restaurant you may default to your 'usual meal' and find yourself having to consciously remind yourself to look at vegetarian options. Another example may be that you change jobs, yet while distracted you find yourself on autopilot, taking your old journey to your former employment.

Inner Doubt? Kick It Out!

We want to help you think positively and create a supportive inner voice.

Your brain is just like a computer: if you put good information in, then you will get good information out. Making affirmations and incantations is quite simple, and once you have made them, if you repeat them daily you will start to think and subsequently feel different.

Incantations must be in the present tense for the best results.

Write out any of the negative thoughts, beliefs or phrases that are limiting you. For example, you might say:

A 'I don't have the time.'

B 'I'm always tired.'

C 'I don't have enough money.'

D 'I'm just depressed.'

Once you have the negative statements or phrases written out, replace the phrases with something more positive and empowering. This is often just the opposite of the negative belief or phrase. Here are some positive replacements for the limiting beliefs mentioned:

A 'Time is equal to all. We all get twenty-four hours each day and I always make time for what I'm committed to.'

B 'I can be energetic and full of life! I can change my physiology and create energy in an instant.'

C 'I can find a way to make money. I am resourceful.'

D 'I am happy because I can choose to be happy right now.'

Here is a list of affirmations and incantations that we have used in the past, to give you some further ideas.

Once you have your personal list, say your incantations as often as you wish – out loud if possible – and as you say them, really feel the statements resonating within your body. Totally and utterly own them.

* **What I do now shapes my today and helps create my tomorrow.**
* **The past does not equal the future.**
* **Problems always pass.**
* **I love my life!**
* **All I need is within me right now.**
* **Life doesn't happen to me, it happens for me.**
* **The best is yet to come.**
* **I love myself for who I am.**
* **I am grateful for every moment of my life.**
* **I am totally and fully comfortable with who I am.**
* **Life is a gift that I enjoy every day.**
* **The more I look for good, the more good comes to me.**
* **I control how I feel and can change my state in an instant.**
* **My home is a warm, happy place that supports my wellbeing.**
* **I am always at peace.**
* **I am blessed with a beautiful family.**
* **I accomplish anything I put my mind to.**
* **If I am committed, there is always a way.**
* **My thoughts are positive and optimistic.**

* If doubt comes in, I change my thoughts and kick it out.

* I learn from every experience in my life.

* I live in the present and live well.

* If I eat healthy, I know I will be healthy.

* Good words in make good words come out.

A Positive Inner Voice

When you learn to love, respect and care for yourself the positive effects are vast. You will benefit from feeling happier, more optimistic, more enthusiastic, excited to try new things, more sociable and able to chat and make new friends. Furthermore, increased confidence can help reduce anxiety and boost your immune system.

Numerous studies have shown indisputable links between having a positive outlook and improved health. As explained by Julie Axelrod on Psych Central, 'No one really understands how or why a positive attitude helps people recover faster from surgery or cope better with serious diseases – diseases as serious as cancer, heart disease, and AIDS. But mounting evidence suggests that these effects may have something to do with the mind's power over the immune system.'[8]

Similarly, as you feel more worthy, you are more likely to invest in yourself and therefore feel more motivated to exercise and eat healthily. As your natural levels of happiness increase, the need for feel-good crutches such as sweet foods and alcohol can also diminish. It is hardly surprising, therefore, that this book, and taking the necessary actions shared to inflate your confidence and self-esteem, can also lead to benefits such as:

* Lower blood pressure

* Healthier weight

* More balanced blood-sugar levels

* Improved immunity

* Better mobility

* Healthier heart

* Increased longevity

* Less anxiety and stress

* Better sleep

Positive thinking helps with stress management and can even improve your health.

Mayo Clinic[9]

Recap

Go back to Chapter 3 and look through your self-esteem questionnaire (see page 46). Has anything changed or improved since working through this chapter? Have you identified some of the negative stories you have been telling yourself?

Consider healthier self-talk and affirmations to repeat in response to each of the statements listed in the questionnaire, so as to present yourself with more positive evidence in answer to each statement.

For example, statement 1:

At times I think I am no good at all.

(There have been many times when I have been more than good enough, such as when I did a kind act for my friend.)

Finally, reflect on your timeline (see page 18). Can you add some more positive life events? Could you consider your interpretation of some of the negatives in a slightly more positive way?

For example:

My parents divorced.

(My parents divorced each other, not me.)

Thank you for everything. You have helped me more than you'll ever know.

Hazel

5

Confidence Saboteurs

I attended your workshop and wanted to say thank you. The day was so informative and inspiring and exactly what I needed to help me address my self-esteem issues.

I found the timeline exercise so enlightening, it has helped me explain why I feel the way I do. I already feel lighter from realisations the timeline highlighted to me.

Thank you for giving me the tools to move forward and achieve the life I want.

Warmest thanks.

Sophie

We often use the analogy that the brain is like a computer. A brand-new computer has immense capacity and capability but holds minimal programs. The quality of the programs that are installed in the computer will be influenced by the creator of the programs and the information installed. Exactly the same is true of your brain, though instead of programs you are installing schemas.

Would you trust a four-year-old child to input all the complex systems that you need in order to run your new computer? Probably not, and yet so many of us have brains that have been programmed with inaccurate negative schemas that were created in childhood, when we lacked the capability to analyse whether they were true or false.

For example, if you were repeatedly told as a child that you were unlovable, that will have created a negative schema that may well still affect you today. Even though you are perfectly lovable and worthy of care and attention, you may be operating on an old program that you have not challenged since it was first installed. It may feel like 'the truth' to you, rather than just something you have learned.

As you go through life, programs are constantly installed and others are upgraded as your knowledge and experience grows. An example of this would be your reading schema, which improves with practice as your skill develops through school.

Unfortunately, some of these programs are updated detrimentally as additional negative evidence and information is applied. An example of this is someone who is bullied at school. Each time they are bullied, the bullying schema is cultivated and reinforced, leaving the victim believing more and more that they are worthless or deserving of this unacceptable behaviour. As long as these negative programs remain unchallenged, and no contrary positive evidence is accepted, the unhelpful negative program or schema continues to run as a background operating system.

Programs or schemas are installed consciously and unconsciously. Some schemas are installed by choice (for example, learning to drive) and others you have no control over, such as your accent. Some you install yourself, and some are installed by others. Some are installed with accurate factual information, others with inaccurate and compromised information. It is for this reason that no two people are identical; even if they have had identical experiences, their reactions will have been different.

> *We are as beautiful, as confident and as intelligent as the words we choose to use to describe ourselves.*

Who You Are

Your opinion of yourself and your abilities is as accurate and sophisticated as the capabilities of the age you were when you created it. If you have never stopped to question how and why you feel the way you do, you may be operating on an opinion of yourself that was established many decades earlier, and which doesn't take into account all of your achievements and learnings since. Or you may be operating on an opinion of yourself that is actually someone else's opinion.

So much of our perception of who we are and what we are capable of is based upon how other people have made us feel. This means that a vital element of addressing a lack of confidence is to address your confidence saboteurs: those people whose actions and words may have created negative schemas in your brain. It is important to understand that these saboteurs may not have intended to cause you harm by their actions. We are influenced not only by their actions, but by how we interpreted these life-altering events and any misinterpretations we may have made, especially when very young.

> *See it for what it was, and not how it felt.*

Your schemas can also be considered as the 'confidence programs' that have been installed in our brains. It is possible that your confidence programs have been corrupted by a confidence saboteur or saboteurs. Installed with inaccurate information, they have sat in your unconscious mind, directing how you think and feel when facing any situation where confidence is required. This inaccurate schema, together with the spokesperson (your inner voice), convinces you of your impending and certain failure, convincing you to 'flee' or 'freeze' in preparation to be embarrassed and severely judged. It is at this moment that your internal protection mechanism jumps to your aid, except it often makes things worse, leading to issues such as social anxiety and glossophobia, which is a fear of public speaking.

Internal Protection Mechanism

When being asked or expected to perform something that is completely out of your comfort zone, or to enter a situation where you expect to be humiliated, your protection mechanism is pushed into action. Your body wants to protect you from a situation it perceives as distressing. When faced with worrying triggers, feelings of anxiety are normal, and in real-life threatening situations they are essential for your survival. This human protection system is commonly known as the 'fight-or-flight' response, and is sometimes referred to as 'fight, flight or freeze', which may all sound familiar when you have been put on the spot, in a situation where confidence is required.

To protect us from real dangers, the fight-or-flight response releases adrenaline. Adrenaline primes the body to fight for a short period, by creating a burst of energy to protect us from a threat.

Equally, adrenaline enables us to flee with faster-than-usual reaction times and a speed we couldn't otherwise achieve or sustain. The dose of adrenaline increases the heart rate, which pumps our oxygenated blood around the body faster. It also stimulates faster breathing, to increase oxygen levels in our bloodstream and provide our limbs with the extra energy necessary to fight or flee from danger. This can often make your limbs feel heavy and you feel lightheaded if you do not act on this heightened adrenaline. You may recall some of these feelings from times when an expectation of a confident display has been needed from you.

The freeze response occurs before deciding to take flight. Most mammals freeze for a few milliseconds to assess the situation. Or you may find yourself unable to act at all, freezing mid-sentence, for example.

We often refer to these feelings as anxiety.

It's important to acknowledge that anxiety is entirely normal. The ability to create anxiety is something that has existed in humans since we were cavemen and women. It was an essential and often life-saving mechanism designed to protect us from dangers, such as ferocious wild animals. Simply put, it's our evolutionary survival tool.

We now live in a world where we are mostly safe from ferocious animals and for most of us it's rare to encounter actual physical danger. As a result, anxiety is being triggered by situations that are emotionally challenging but not life-threatening, such as carrying out a speech, attending a job interview or asking someone on a date.

The fight-or-flight response is often being inappropriately activated during normal, everyday situations when facing issues such as work worries, money concerns, family and health issues, which demand our attention without necessarily requiring the fight-or-flight reaction.

The symptoms of the fight-or-flight response caused by the spike in our stress hormone, adrenaline, are varied and numerous, but most people will experience some of the following, which you may be familiar with:

* Increased heart rate or sense of heart palpitations
* Over-breathing (hyperventilating)
* Shaking
* Muscle tension
* Tension and tightness, or sense of compression, in the chest
* Feeling hot
* Feeling sweaty and clammy
* Heaviness or numbness in the arms and legs
* Tingling sensation in the arms and legs
* Numbness or tingling in the face
* Nausea
* Flatulence
* A need to use the toilet more often
* Headache
* Dry mouth
* Hypervigilance
* Hypersensitivity
* Light-headedness

To sever the link from your internal protection mechanism to your confidence schema, it is essential that you locate and upgrade the corrupt schema or program by challenging the quality of the instillation, the installer or your confidence saboteur(s).

Finding the Foundation

Knowing that we are neither born with or without confidence helps us to understand that lacking in confidence is a learned behaviour. Our aim is to help you find the original learning that created the foundation on which your lack of confidence has been built. This learning can be acquired through:

1 Copying behaviour

Our parents are our first role models in life. Just as we copy their accents, we will also copy their behaviours, mannerisms, terminology, palate, worries and also anxieties. This means that if a parent, or other significant adult in your developmental years, lacked confidence, there is a high probability you will display some of those traits of low confidence, too.

2 Believing what we're told

A question we often pose to our clients in the clinic is, 'How do you know what your name is?' For example, if your name is Siobhan or David, how do you know that? Who told you? This is most likely something that you have never considered before, yet it can be incredibly relevant.

Children are often instructed by their parents not to speak to strangers. Yet, when we are in therapy we often discover an early event or memory when a parent introduces their child to an adult or even a group of adults (such as a shopkeeper, a doctor, a stranger on the bus, the parents' work colleagues, etc.) when this complete stranger may ask the child a question. The child often does not respond. The lack of response can be as a result of conflict, such as, 'Do I speak or do I not? Is this a stranger?' Alternatively, perhaps the child does not understand the question posed, or perhaps this adult even looks scary to this small child.

However, as the child momentarily becomes mute, the parent will hurriedly offer the adult trying to engage in a conversation an acceptable response, such as, 'So sorry, *my little one is shy.*'

Just as your parents told you your name, your parent can also inadvertently and without any intention or malice give you the label of 'shy', which you carry forever if left unchallenged. All a possible consequence of a childhood misunderstanding.

3 Being spoken for

If you are a younger sibling, the chances are you may have 'been spoken for'.

In an effort to highlight their position as the eldest, an older sibling may have made decisions on your behalf, resulting in you believing from a young age that your opinions and choices do not matter or are not valid.

Further, if you are a younger sibling by a substantial gap, your older sibling may have taken a parental role in an endeavour to protect their little brother or sister. This can result in the older sibling speaking on your behalf with a nurturing intention, but this can cause a younger sibling to feel they have less of a voice or a value than the older child. It can also mean the younger sibling doesn't have the opportunity to develop their social skills, as they are spoken for and overprotected, instead of having chances to build their confidence through interactions.

Finally, a 2019 study by Naomi Havron et al. found that children with an older brother are more likely to experience a delay with their speech development.[10] Researchers speculated that older sisters interact with younger siblings, helping them speak earlier, while older brothers are less inclined to speak to a younger child. Issues with speech can knock a child's confidence, even more so if noted by a parent and misinterpreted as shyness, or worse still something that is not normal. Some children are even scolded for their lack of speech, creating a schema that causes them to believe their efforts to talk are unacceptable. The child can then become nervous, feeling judged when speaking, even in adulthood.

4 Trauma

Trauma encompasses any situation in which you have ever felt distressed. In your childhood and developmental years, any traumatic situations that happened as you were first learning to interact with the world will have had an impact on your confidence. Children are incredibly impressionable. Situations that created emotions such as embarrassment, humiliation and even guilt, that resulted in you being reprimanded or punished, or that left you feeling vulnerable or inadequate, believing your actions caused disappointment or embarrassment to someone else, can create negative schemas that stay with you well into adulthood.

As well as being impressionable, children do not have the life experience or the cognitive ability to calmly and dispassionately evaluate a situation, particularly as the distress of a trauma is often sudden. This can mean that we adopt a schema that is distorted, because the information we have internalised is incorrect – such as, 'My father left me,' rather than, 'My father left my mother.'

So although your conscious mind says, 'I want to be confident,' your old negative schemas may hold you back, while your fight-or-flight response tries to protect you with symptoms of anxiety.

What Does This Mean to Me?

No matter what situation we face, our unconscious mind is always asking the question: 'What does this mean to me?'

Our response to this question, and our subsequent behaviour, will be based on the information we receive via our schemas, which have been created from our life experiences.

This information feedback dictates our behaviour. So if we experience a trauma or copy a behaviour as a child, we can only evaluate the situation from a child's perspective, with a child's limited life experience. This is why, even though as an adult you might know your confidence issues hold you back, you can't help behaving like the child that initially created the protection schema to keep you safe from further trauma, humiliation or pain. Unless your protection schema is conditioned, you will still be acting from the point of view of a wounded child. Our work helps you to 'upgrade' the original event so that it can be seen from an adult perspective and viewed in a more positive and accurate manner.

Of course, this means identifying the original traumatising event in the first place.

All the things that happened to me, I now realise were not personal to me. This has now freed me from sixty years of a burden I carried.

I feel lighter and am so amazed how it happened. I feel wonderful. You have a gift to be able to heal people of their negative thoughts.

My sincere thanks.

Carol

Saboteurs

It is difficult to fix or address anything that you do not fully understand. Imagine trying to complete a thousand-piece jigsaw puzzle, without having any knowledge of the picture you are trying to create. This is potentially the situation that you have been in until now when it comes to building your confidence. You have the pieces, and some knowledge of what needs to be done, but no format to follow, which makes it difficult to slot the pieces into place. With that in mind, we would now like to help you gain a clearer picture of how to put your puzzle together by considering your confidence saboteurs.

Parents

As we previously stated, our parents are our first role models in life. How they speak to us, how they treat us, how they help us and interact with us are all components in shaping how our self-belief develops in childhood. As explained by University of Nebraska-Lincoln, 'Children are born without social knowledge or social skills, and they eagerly look for someone to imitate. That "someone" is usually one or both parents. Parents are a child's first teachers and role models. And usually children are more affected by what their parents do than by what their parents say.'[11]

It may be that our parents were openly harsh and critical, or even abusive. Often, however, it is the case that a child's own interpretation of events can be very wrong through simple misunderstanding.

CASE STUDY
Joan: Low Self-worth

Joan was a sixty-two-year-old lady who had lost both her husband and her mother in recent years. She came to see us in our private clinic telling us that she felt 'lost, helpless and hopeless'.

Having read her self-esteem questionnaire (similar to the one we shared with you earlier, see page 46), it was evident that Joan had rock-bottom confidence and very low self-esteem. And it wasn't surprising, as her timeline of challenging life experiences ran to over fifty pages.

Joan used words such as 'pathetic' and 'useless' to describe herself. She was very quiet, had rounded shoulders and constantly looked down. We asked Joan what she would want from us if anything were possible. Joan said, 'I want a voice, a voice that speaks with confidence and not one that feels inadequate and foolish.' She went on to say, 'I honestly don't think I add any value to this world, and no one, not even my children, likes me.' This was both heartbreaking and difficult to hear, when it was evident that Joan was such a lovely lady.

We started to work our way through the negative events on Joan's timeline. Most were incidents from her childhood, including regrets for not having tried things, accepted opportunities or spoken out for herself. This pattern continued to the very day she sat in front of us.

We explained to Joan that we are all a product of our environment, and we wanted to understand more about her childhood. Joan shared that she had an older sister, and that she had grown up with a very strict father. Joan believed that she had been an inconvenience, and that her father was disappointed by her, both for being the person she was and also for not being a boy. She said that, as children, she and her sister were constantly told not to make a noise or to speak. Their mother threatened that any noise would be punished by their father. Joan said she spent most of her childhood in her bedroom, reading.

Joan described her father as a terrifying figure, who had no patience and who felt that nothing she did was ever good enough. Even when she passed the entrance exam for the local grammar school he had not congratulated her. Joan also appeared bitter that the grammar school had been well outside of their social class and yet they insisted on sending her there. Joan said she had been laughed at throughout her entire education and made to feel like an outcast by the other girls due to her second-hand and homemade uniform.

We asked Joan why she had the accent that she had. Joan said, 'Because of where I come from.' We asked her how she had learned her accent. Joan replied that she had copied her parents. We then asked, 'How did your dad learn how to be a dad?' Joan had never considered this before, but then went on to say that no doubt he had learned from his own father, who she said had been a stereotypical strict Victorian father who showed no love or emotion. Joan was starting to realise that her father was merely copying his own father's behaviour and that his strict parenting was not a reflection on her. We asked Joan whether she believed her father had become strict because of her or because of his role model of fatherhood. She, of course, said it was because of her grandfather. We pointed out to Joan that it was quite sad that her father had not been able to experience emotion and it had not been his fault. Joan agreed and said she was feeling quite sorry for her father in hindsight.

We spoke about perspective and asked Joan what she believed had been the criteria of a good father back in Victorian times. Joan responded, 'To provide a roof over your head, food in your belly and an education.' We asked if this was also likely to be her father's criteria. Joan said that it was, and that her own father had fulfilled *his* criteria of being a good dad. We asked Joan why her father may have wanted to be a good dad. As tears welled in her eyes, she said, 'Because he loved us and showed it in the only way he knew how.'

With this realisation there was an immediate change in Joan's demeanour. It was as if a light had been switched on, and the little girl's views were being superseded by Joan the adult's as things started to fall into place.

Joan shared how she would hear her parents brag about her having made it to grammar school. She also shared that her father had worked from home, and despite money being tight, he had worked extra hard to ensure she could travel to the grammar school and that she had a good education, which meant that her parents had to cut corners with the homemade and second-hand uniform. We asked Joan, 'Was the second-hand uniform intended to punish you or was it actually a reflection of how loved you were?' Joan replied, 'Oh my goodness, they loved me so much they did everything they had to, to get me there.'

We then asked Joan about being told to be quiet at home. Why might that have been? Was that because they did not want to hear her voice? Or was it because Dad was trying to work, to fulfil his role and criteria of a good dad? Again, Joan confirmed, 'It's because he loved us.'

We asked Joan if she had been loved. She said, 'Yes.' We asked if her father had been proud of her. She said, 'Yes.' Although there were numerous events we had to address with Joan, her low self-esteem, her lack of self-value and the belief that she had been silenced as no one had wanted to listen to her had been positively challenged and lifted. Joan's confidence and self-esteem schemas had been positively conditioned, allowing her to now build on her confidence without a pessimistic voice holding her back.

Parents – a positive perspective

Most parents are trying, and doing, their best. Of course, we can all find some area of criticism when it comes to considering our own parents' capabilities, or indeed those of others, but we must not lose sight of our parents as flawed individuals who learned to parent from their own parents. Our parents' failings are not to spite or hurt us. Unless they have really examined their own past, they will only know, and re-enact, what they have previously witnessed.

As we saw with Joan's story, it is easy for a child to misunderstand or misinterpret a situation, and this misinterpretation can influence us forevermore unless positively challenged.

We often hear clients say that they could never do anything right as children, that they felt their best was never good enough as their parents were constantly critical of their efforts. Growing up with criticism can leave a lasting impression, with a child creating a negative schema that even their best is not good enough. But it is possible to look at this in a different, more positive way. Perhaps a more accurate reading of this situation would be that this parent loved their child so much they were trying to give them every chance to be the best they could be. Although it may have backfired, this behaviour is an act of absolute love to help better their child.

Ultimately, the key to letting go of parental issues in relation to your confidence is to accept that your parents' approach was not personal to you, or a result of your failings as an individual. Perhaps their parenting was antiquated, perhaps it was too severe or critical, but their approach was not intended to punish you. Their parenting techniques were a consequence and a reflection of their own upbringing. If your parent or parents had truly not cared, they would not have ensured that you had a roof over your head, food on the table or an education.

When we can forgive our parents, it becomes easier to forgive ourselves.

'Children need role models rather than critics.'
Joseph Joubert[12]

Siblings

Just as we do not choose our parents, neither do we choose our siblings, who can prove to be our very best friends or our worst enemies. Sibling solidarity can provide strength, belonging and certainty, yet sibling rivalry can be painful and destructive. Comparison, jealousy and favouritism can all contribute to sibling rivalry, as well as whether you are the eldest, middle or youngest child.

CASE STUDY
Louise: Imposter Syndrome

The confident, attractive, successful woman who sat before us in our clinic did not reflect the person that we had expected from her pre-therapy questionnaire. When we asked Louise why she needed our help she said, 'Because I am a serious fraud.'

Louise went on to tell us that, despite having been an 'A' student throughout her life, excelling in her studies and having a great job, she was awash with anxiety due to an expectation that she would be 'found out'. While others believed in her, looked up to her even, Louise felt she was not good enough, and that her outward persona was all an illusion. She simply did not believe she was good enough, and the confidence she seemed to display was just a very convincing act.

From her questionnaire, we had a very good idea of why Louise felt this way. But our work is not about telling, it is about helping individuals reach their own realisations.

Louise was the eldest of two girls, with a three-year age gap between her and her younger sister. Louise recalls growing up feeling that, despite being a high achiever academically, she was just never good enough. She went on to say that her parents would point out her sister's positive attributes over hers. She told us, 'I was always the clever one, but then my mum and dad would always default to "but our Lorna is a great gymnast", "our Lorna has a lovely singing voice", "our Lorna is creative" and I could just never compete.' Louise felt that no matter what she did, her sister was and would always be the shining light.

We asked Louise whether she and her sister went to different schools. Louise confirmed that they both attended a private school, but that Lorna had failed the compulsory entrance exam to go on to the senior school and had instead attended the local high school.

We asked Louise whether her immediate family had all known that Louise was at the private school. She confirmed that they did. We asked Louise whether her immediate family had all known that her sister had not made it through to the senior school? She confirmed that they did.

We asked about her parents' friends. Did they have kids? And what schools did they attend? Louise was a little confused about our questioning, but confirmed that most of her parents' friends were either close relatives or the parents of people at Louise's school.

We then asked Louise, 'What do you think the other parents from your school may have thought about your sister Lorna failing the entrance exam, knowing that all their own children had passed?'

Louise went silent. Her eye movements were evidence to us that she was starting to see things more accurately from an adult's perspective.

We asked, 'Louise, why do you think your parents had to constantly talk about your sister's achievements and qualities?' After a few moments, Louise looked down and said, 'OMG! Because everyone already knew mine!'

With our help, Louise was able to see, for the very first time, that the reason her parents had praised her sister so often was because so many people complimented Louise, so they did this to protect her sister's self-worth.

As the realisation started to sink in, Louise said, 'Poor Lorna.' As a mum, Louise completely realised how she had misunderstood the situation. She had failed to remember the numerous times her parents sat at prize-givings or parents' evenings smiling at her with pride.

Louise was flabbergasted that she had blocked out this point of view before. We asked Louise, 'Do you think your parents were proud of you?' Louise replied, 'Of course,' and then said, 'In fact, as an adult, they tell me all the time how proud they are, but I have rejected their compliments and not believed them.'

We finally asked about her current work position, in which she had told us at the start of the session she felt like a fraud.

Our question to Louise was, 'How did you get this job?' She went on to tell us that it was due to her employment experience and results. We asked, 'Were you the only applicant?' She said, 'Of course not, there were hundreds.' We asked, 'So did you get given the job out of pity?' Louise replied, 'No.'

We asked about the person who had interviewed her, who Louise described as someone successful and experienced. We asked, 'So who did the successful and experienced CEO believe to be the best person for the job?' Louise gave us the biggest smile and said, 'Me.' We concluded with, 'Are you a fraud, Louise?' She said with confidence, 'No, I am not.'

Outer confidence is often a shield to hide the fearful person within.

Siblings – a positive perspective

It is common for children to believe their sibling is favoured by a parent, which can lead to a child feeling inadequate. This experience, whether the child is correct or not, can then result in them forming a schema that they are not good enough, which can impact their self-worth and confidence forevermore.

The truth is that one child may get on better with one parent, perhaps due to having common interests, but this does not mean that the level of love is different.

To extinguish any lasting detrimental effect of a belief that a sibling was loved more than you, it is important to acknowledge that the kind of love parents show to each of their children will never be the same, because no two children are identical.

Partner

Falling in love is undoubtedly one of the most wonderful, intoxicating feelings that we as human beings are able to experience. A loving partner can enhance our life, our happiness and our self-esteem. Yet falling in love with someone who turns out to be controlling or abusive can also change a once-confident person into someone who becomes a shadow of their former self.

It is estimated that police in England and Wales receive over 100 calls relating to domestic abuse every hour. And yet statistics of the prevalence of domestic abuse are most likely severely understated, due to victims being afraid to come forward. There is also a misconception that domestic abuse relates only to violence, while it actually encompasses verbal and emotional abuse, coercion, bullying and control, too. These forms of abuse can be as painful and damaging as physical violence.

CASE STUDY
Gail: Feeling Fat and Ugly

Gail was a truly beautiful lady. Her kindness and compassion were clear to see on her lovely smiling face when we welcomed her into our clinic.

It saddened us to hear Gail describe herself as fat, ugly, a disgrace and an embarrassment to her family, both for the way she looked and her inability to speak out or grasp any opportunities that came her way.

Gail told us that she had grown up in a home where her father was in charge. No one crossed him, not even her mother. They would quake with fear if he became angry or if she and her siblings made too much noise. Although he was a good provider, Gail would often observe her mum's subservience to her father, and would witness him being nasty, angry and controlling towards her. As a consequence of her conditioning, assuming this subservient behaviour was normal, Gail was overly tolerant of others being unkind or harsh towards her. Her learning or schema was that, in the face of aggression, she should retreat and say nothing.

When Gail was fourteen, she met her first love, who went on to be her husband. They went on to have three wonderful children. Once they were married and living together, she became aware that her husband was quite controlling, and she did her best to appease him. She would make excuses for his behaviour when he did not allow her to wear certain clothes that he felt were inappropriate for her, and also when he forbade her to go out and socialise with her friends.

Gail was lonely, as, while her husband had a good social life, she was left at home caring for their three very young children. Gail turned to food for comfort and company.

After eleven years of marriage, she noticed he was

spending less time at home. He began to pay more attention to his appearance and his criticism of Gail accelerated, making Gail eat more. As she gained weight her husband would berate and humiliate her, calling her vile names.

Not only was her husband being unkind to her, but at that time her father was also terminally ill, so she could not even look to her mum for support. She felt incredibly lonely. The only 'friend' Gail had to talk to was another mother at the school gates, who she really appreciated. Gail confided in her friend about how she felt her marriage was failing, only then to discover a text message on her husband's phone from her school-gate friend, thanking him for the afternoon of passion they had just shared.

Gail felt like her world had completely fallen apart; two of the only people she thought she could rely on and trust had totally let her down. As soon as the affair was revealed, her husband left and Gail now spent each night at home alone, comfort eating, but after six years of being single, Gail joined an online dating site and soon started chatting with a man, who turned out to be lovely and amazing – so much so that three years later she married him.

Gail's new husband was a lovely man. He was kind and attentive and would pay her many compliments, which she would hear, yet never, ever believe were true.

We asked Gail to tell us what she saw when she looked in a full-length mirror. As expected, the words that Gail used to describe herself were very disrespectful. She used words such as 'fat cow', 'weak', 'pathetic', 'disgusting', 'disgraceful', 'pathetic', 'weak-willed' and 'an embarrassment'. We did not believe that these words were her own; she was using the words of others and how other people had made her feel to describe herself. It was heartbreaking.

We asked how her first marriage had made her feel. She told us it made her feel very embarrassed and ashamed. Everyone seemed to know about the affair except for her, and they were no doubt laughing at her behind her back. Gail became upset and said that she had failed in her marriage, failed to lose weight and she was failing as a wife currently, as even though she loved her husband, she couldn't lose weight even for him. It was clear to see that the word 'failed' was likely to be the cause of Gail's issues.

We explained to Gail that the reason why she felt she was failing was because she believed she was a failure, and while believing she was destined to fail, nothing was worth trying, hence her lack of motivation. Gail agreed.

We asked about the vows she had made in church to her first husband. When Gail repeated them, we asked her if she had failed to honour her marriage vows. Gail confirmed that she hadn't. It was her husband who cheated and left her. Again, we asked her whether she had failed in her marriage. Gail said no.

We then asked what she believed would constitute a good husband or wife. Gail used words such as 'loyal', 'kind', 'caring', 'loving', 'supportive' and 'giving'. We asked if she had fulfilled each of those roles as we repeated the words she had used. She confirmed she had.

It was refreshing to witness Gail, unprompted, start to tell us how she was a very loyal wife and, had her husband not had the affair, she would have stayed by his side forevermore, despite his disrespectful, controlling behaviour. Gail said, 'I did not fail as a wife.' As she said this with conviction, we moved on to address her life now.

We asked Gail whether her husband gave her compliments. She told us her new husband gave her compliments all the time.

We asked Gail whether her husband was a good man. Gail confirmed that he was one of the nicest human beings she had ever met. We asked whether her husband was a liar, whereby she looked a little offended on his behalf, and told us, 'Of course not.' We asked Gail, 'If your husband isn't a liar, why do you offend him and essentially call him a liar every time he gives you a compliment?' Gail replied by saying she didn't. We pointed out that she did, and that she was being disrespectful, as she had told us that her husband gave her compliments on a daily basis, yet she did not believe them, therefore in essence she was calling him a liar.

Gail was dumbfounded by this and was experiencing enormous conflict, as she knew her husband was not a liar, yet she had no confidence in herself. We asked Gail whether she would ever intentionally be unkind to her husband. She said, 'Never.' We explained that whenever her husband would give her a compliment and she didn't believe him, this was disrespectful and tantamount to calling him a liar, whereas the polite thing to do would be to say, 'Thank you.'

We explained to Gail that a compliment is like being given a gift, and as much as we understood that it might be difficult for her to accept it because of her low self-esteem, all she had to do was say, 'Thank you.' Simply saying thank you starts a new habit, and helps to start building self-esteem. Gail agreed, saying that she had never considered that before.

To conclude our session, we asked Gail to look in the mirror – a process we will share with you later in the book (see page 220). Gail confirmed that she felt so much better about herself. She told us that she had a nice personality and a pretty face, that she was an achiever, having brought up three children on her own, and that despite the challenges in her life, she had a good job, her three children adored her and her husband loved her.

Partner – a positive perspective

If you are in an abusive relationship, our advice to you would be to talk to someone you trust, your doctor or a domestic abuse charity who can offer you help and support without judgement.

Domestic abuse is against the law because it is wrong. The perpetrator of this abuse is fully aware that their actions are unacceptable, hence why they hide their actions behind closed doors and deflect responsibility by blaming their victim. Violence is never acceptable and you will never be judged by those who are there to help you. On the contrary, domestic abuse charities are there to support you and offer as little or as much assistance as you need. They can even steer your partner in the right direction to obtain help for their behaviour.

Before meeting Nik, I, Eva, was in an abusive relationship, and understand how the progressive grooming and abuse makes you feel. Although you are the victim, you are manipulated to believe that you are at fault and have antagonised them to behave in the way they do, and thus you feel ashamed. Equally, you are made to believe that you cannot live or exist without them, and you believe their promises that they will change. The truth is, they will never change. Imagine if what is happening to you were happening to your best friend, sister or child. Consider the advice you would give them, and take it for yourself. The truth is that to have gone through what you have endured is a testament to your strength, loyalty and value. Walk out, speak out and ask for help. I did, and like many others I have spoken to, it was only then that I found true happiness and my true love.

If a current or ex-partner has tried to put you down for any reason, then please realise that despite the derogatory comments they made about you, they chose you as their partner! They chose you because they wanted to be with you, they were attracted to you, and they were happy to introduce you to their friends and loved ones. Happy, not embarrassed, regardless of what their insecurities may have led them to say about you!

Furthermore, consider why they tried to put you down. This is usually because they realise that in some way you are superior to them, and they are worried you will leave or they will lose you to someone else. They therefore say and do things to clip your wings and stop them from losing you. It is a twisted need to shatter your confidence to make you feel more needy of them.

Please trust us when we tell you that your sparkle shone so bright that your ex-partner felt inadequate, and this is why they tried to diminish it.

In order for you to move on with confidence, it is important that you accept that your abusive ex did not behave in the way they did because of you. They were an abuser or a bully before you met them, and nothing you did made them that way. Pure and simple, they are an abuser or bully and, unless they get help, they will continue to be: this behaviour is a consequence of their own past and not anything you did.

See our Bungee Technique later in this chapter (see page 124) to help cut your emotional ties to your ex, and our Mirror Technique (see page 220) to appreciate your immense value.

> ***You have the power and the right to state, 'This is not how my story is going to end.'***

Bully

A significant number of the hundreds of people who have come to us with issues relating to low confidence have been the victims of bullying.

It is hardly surprising that bullies are the most prolific confidence saboteurs, because there are so many opportunities for us to be bullied in life. A bully can be a parent, sibling, fellow school pupil, work colleague, partner, neighbour or team leader. We may come to feel that we deserve to be bullied, due to how the bullying makes us question our worth. We then begin to bully ourselves, internalising the bullying that we have experienced and turning it onto ourselves in the form of the inner critic we explored earlier.

Any form of bullying is an emotionally damaging act, often leaving the victim feeling inadequate, unworthy and lacking in confidence. Furthermore, the victim can experience self-loathing and low self-esteem and go on to self-harm, self-medicate with food or alcohol, or self-punish by holding back from achieving or venturing to fulfil true dreams, desires and abilities.

The bully, on the other hand, can go through life often unaware of the damage their actions have caused, not giving their victim a second thought. We hope that, if the behaviour of a bully has destroyed your confidence, this book and our techniques will help you transform from victim to victor.

> *Bullies have been referred to as being like sand paper. Their scratch may hurt, but you end up polished and they end up useless.*

CASE STUDY
Gary: Self-hatred

We met Gary when he attended one of our workshops and bravely raised his hand when we requested a volunteer for our confidence demonstration.

He spoke about his lack of self-worth and how he totally hated himself. As Gary spoke about the life he had endured, the majority of the room began to cry. Gary was just three years old when his mum died, and his memories of her were quite vague, including details of how she died. It wasn't until his twenties that he learned she had had cancer and that by the time it was discovered, it was too late to save her.

Gary and his four older brothers were left with their dad, who was working full-time to keep a roof over their heads. Not long after his wife's death, Gary's father married again. Looking back, Gary felt that it was likely that his father quickly remarried to provide a mother and carer for his children. However, Gary went on to describe her as the stereotypical wicked stepmother from fairy tales.

He recalls his stepmother taunting him and his brothers with cakes, while refusing to let them have any. Gary had a vivid memory of waking in the night when he was perhaps eight or nine years of age, feeling incredibly hungry. He went downstairs to the kitchen and took some biscuits, but his stepmother woke and chastised him, twisting and pinching his skin, and telling him that he was disgusting and fat.

From then on, Gary's stepmother seemed to target him, bullying him at every possible opportunity when his father was not home.

Gary recalls his stepmother cruelly telling him, many times, that his mother hadn't really died, but had left the family because she hated Gary. When Gary was twelve or thirteen, she told him that his mother had actually committed suicide because of her hatred of Gary. He grew up feeling loathed and confused. Although his dad was a kind and quiet soul, Gary did not feel able to talk to him about his stepmother or his own mother.

The moment Gary was old enough, he left school so he could earn money to get away and gain some control over his life. He vowed he would never go hungry again. Because he had previously been restricted around food, Gary started to overeat. Having no confidence thanks to his stepmother's bullying, he kept himself to himself and did not venture into having a relationship. He believed that he was fat, ugly and would never, ever find or deserve love.

Gary had created schemas in childhood based on the belief that his mum had left him because he wasn't good enough. Even though in adulthood he learned the truth about his mother's cancer from his aunt, he was still being guided by his childhood schemas, which had remained unchallenged. He still felt unworthy and despised.

We asked Gary whether his aunt had any reason to lie to him. Gary said no.

We asked Gary whether he had any memories of his mum being unkind, cruel or dismissing him? Gary told us the memories he had were of a kind and loving mum.

We asked Gary why he was choosing his stepmother over his actual mother. He looked hurt and confused and said, 'I would never choose my stepmother over my own mum.' We pointed out that believing his stepmother's stories over his own loving memories was like him choosing to believe his stepmother over his own mother. We saw an instant and visible shift in Gary when he said, 'I have never looked at it that way before, you are right.'

We then asked Gary, 'Did your mum choose to leave you?' Gary said no. We asked, 'Why do you think your mum had four children?' Gary answered, 'Because she must have wanted us.' We pointed out that after she had had one child, if she didn't want any more, she wouldn't have done, and yet she went on to have another three, proving that she enjoyed being a mum.

We then carried out a demonstration of our Mirror Technique with Gary, which we will share with you later (see page 220), and for the first time, since the age of three, Gary was able to see himself through his mother's eyes. The eyes of true and unconditional love. The room fell silent. It was an emotional and beautiful moment.

Bully – a positive perspective

If you have been bullied or made to feel worthless, ask yourself if that person is still in your life now. If not, why would you want to continue to listen to them? If they made you feel bad, and you continue to think and feel badly of yourself, then please realise that any self-deprecation is like continuing where the bully left off. You are obviously so much better than that. You deserve better than that. Do not keep carrying the memory of the bully with you – they do not deserve that distinction. Please consider that being unkind or making anyone (even yourself) feel bad is not in your nature.

Pity your bully. To be toxic suggests they have come from a toxic, polluted environment. A bully bullies, so although it felt terrible to you, it was not personal, as the bully will have bullied you, others before you and others at the same time, and will continue to bully others in the future.

Bullies are people who generally have low self-worth and low self-esteem. They may have been bullied themselves, so now bully to avoid being a victim, or they may bully to inflate their own status, and therefore their bullying should not be taken personally. Furthermore, bullies only bully people whose qualities outshine theirs! Please therefore realise that you are amazing and your shine obviously must have dazzled them.

If the memory of a past bully continues to make you feel bad or uncomfortable, you can also try our Bungee Technique at the end of this chapter (see page 124) to enable you to distance yourself from them emotionally.

School teacher

As children we are taught to respect our elders, people of authority and most certainly our school teachers. A teacher can often be someone who has been a positive influence in your life and aided your character-building. A teacher can be a parental figure or a person of admiration and respect, who you endeavoured to impress and from whom you sought praise. As children we look to our teachers as a source of wisdom and knowledge, which means that if their actions or influence are negative or cruel, our confidence can be seriously damaged, as we believe they must be acting out of some knowledge of our shortcomings.

Until becoming therapists, we had not appreciated the dramatic impact a teacher could have on someone's confidence and life, both good and bad. However, we have witnessed on multiple occasions the fallout of a flippant comment or throwaway remark, made in a moment of frustration to a child, an error of judgement or even attempted jovial sarcasm by a teacher.

A remark from a teacher – a person perceived to be in an elevated position by a child – can be carried into adulthood with enormous adverse effects. It is important to point out here that we believe that most school teachers are kind, caring, compassionate and eager to teach, and that any errors they make are usually without intention or malice. Please also consider here that everyone can have a bad day when they just do and say the wrong things because of issues or traumas that they have going on in their own lives. But it is our experience that comments such as 'you won't amount to anything', 'you are an idiot' and 'you are a fool', or acts of favouritism, can crush a child. Additionally, being shouted at, being blamed in error or being humiliated in front of their peers as a child can be incredibly harmful to a person's confidence and their ability to interact with others well into adulthood.

CASE STUDY
Alison: Extreme Social Anxiety

Alison's world was shrinking each day. She said that she had never been confident, but her feelings of extreme anxiety and panic attacks were starting to shut her away from the world.

Alison did not socialise; her colleagues no longer invited her to functions as she had declined too many times, so they just stopped asking. She had even lied to her mother about winning a spa break to avoid having to attend the family Christmas gathering. It was at this point that Alison knew she needed help.

When we met Alison, she was timid and fearful. We explained to her that when she said she had 'never' been confident, a more accurate statement would be that she had learned to lack confidence, and that this was most likely due to a childhood event.

As we talked with Alison, she revealed that her panic and extreme discomfort was most prevalent when she was around people. On further discussion, it transpired that she was afraid she would do something to humiliate herself, and this in turn would cause her feelings of panic.

Together, we looked at Alison's timeline and asked her to consider a time, when there were lots of people present, when she may have felt humiliated. Perhaps at school? With this question, suddenly her posture changed. She said there was a day in junior school when she had been for an early-morning dental appointment and was late getting back to school for her first class. As she walked in, the teacher said, 'Thank you for joining us – did you fancy a lie-in this morning?' The whole class roared with laughter; Alison blushed. One of the children then pointed out how red her face had become when she blushed and another called her a beetroot. This then created additional laughter in the classroom.

Watching Alison's discomfort as she merely recalled this story, and having established that prior to this she did not remember being 'shy', we knew it had to be the instigator of her 'no-confidence' schema.

We asked Alison who had caused that feeling of embarrassment. First, she said it was the class, but then she corrected herself: 'Well, actually it was the teacher.' Then we asked, if this situation had involved another child, would she potentially have laughed and done the same as her classmates in order to distract the teacher from what was potentially a boring lesson? Alison confirmed, 'Yes, probably.' We asked her to consider whether she would have laughed out of malice at the child walking in late. She said, 'No.'

We then asked whether there might have been a similar scenario at school where Alison herself had laughed at another child. She said, 'Definitely.'

We asked Alison to try to recall the children she herself had laughed at in school. Did she think badly of them now, or would she expect them to humiliate themselves if she saw them again?

Alison paused and said, 'I have never looked at it like this before. Of course not, I don't even remember anyone specifically, even though I know I did laugh at others in class.'

It was evident that we were making positive progress, and that Alison's schema was now being positively conditioned.

We then asked Alison to consider the role of a teacher, and she confirmed that it is their duty to positively develop a child, rather than to break and humiliate them. In the circumstances, it was Alison's teacher who should have felt embarrassed, knowing the negative effect that his inappropriate comment would have on her. With that, Alison sighed, and we witnessed a huge release.

Over the following months she shared with us her many achievements, including embarking on an evening college course, attending a colleague's baby shower and successfully applying for a promotion at work.

> *To teach is to touch a life forever.*

Teacher – a positive perspective

As children we often put teachers on a pedestal, and as a result they also have the power to nurture and shape us, as well as educate us.

If a teacher's comments or actions have affected you, and after reading about Alison you realise that this event or events continue to affect you in adulthood, then you must challenge that child's viewpoint. The truth is that the teacher you are potentially allowing to destroy your confidence most likely never thinks of you – are they even alive still? As an adult they have no power over you whatsoever, other than the power you have given them in the past, which was from a child's perspective. In order to assist your change, you must start to challenge this power over your thoughts immediately. If you notice a lack of confidence creeping in, take control. Say in your head, or even out loud, 'I am no longer at school.' Challenging your negative thoughts immediately helps with the creation of new neural pathways and subsequently new conditioned behaviours.

You must update the childhood behavioural schema and become the adult, by first acknowledging that the teacher whose words affected you was human. Just like you, they made mistakes; they also would have had weaknesses that you will have been unaware of. Back in school you may have feared this teacher or inflated their power and status, but the truth is that, like anyone else, they will have experienced relationship issues, challenges at home, illness concerns, financial worries, even problems with their own children. You only knew them as a 'teacher', never as the real person with their worries, frustrations or challenges, nor did you know what kind of a day they were having when they behaved the way they did towards you.

What we know for sure is that the teacher did not just single you out; they will have behaved in the same manner with other children. Their reaction or action was not personal to you. Perhaps they were having a bad day, perhaps they were frustrated with the class, perhaps they did not have the truth or details of factual events or perhaps you even reminded them of someone who had hurt them when they were at school. Whatever they were feeling when they hurt your feelings, it was not right of them to take out their frustrations on a child. So let's look at the situation once more.

Who actually made an error of judgement? Who was actually at fault for their unprofessional response/words/actions? You or the teacher?

Who had a duty of care to you?

Who was the adult in this situation?

Who should feel embarrassed?

Knowing a teacher's job is to nurture, who actually failed?

Of course, the answer to all those questions is 'the teacher'. So, considering the above, *who was blameless*?

Of course, it's you!

'In our relationship with children and young people, we are not dealing with mechanical devices that can be quickly repaired, but living beings.'

Jiddu Krishnamurti[13]

Boss

It is estimated that we spend approximately one-third of our life at work. With that in mind, our overall happiness can be significantly influenced by our work and our work colleagues, especially those who are in senior positions to us.

The pressure of keeping our job, and the salary we rely on, can lead to us accepting what in normal situations would be considered unacceptable behaviour and actions from a work colleague, particularly if they are in a managerial or influential position.

For many who already struggle to vocalise their issues due to a lack of confidence, a problematic boss or work colleague can make life even more challenging and can result in the lack of confidence becoming even more severe.

In fact, a critical and demeaning boss or work colleague can actually completely shatter a once-confident person, leading them to feel fragile, useless, worthless and desperately unhappy.

> *Don't be offended if someone criticises you while you're striving for success, as this is likely the only way they can feel valued.*

CASE STUDY
Sue: Lack of Confidence in Decision-making

We met Sue when she came to chat with us at our workshop. There was a kindness and benevolence that came across in her, yet there was a burning sadness in her eyes.

Sue gave a brief summary of her life. She said her children had grown up, she had left an unhappy marriage and she had taken her first step to financial freedom by getting a job as a carer.

Sue absolutely loved her job and the fact that she was able to add a little sparkle to the lives of the elderly people she cared for. She would often linger after her shift to chat to the residents and their relatives.

Despite the positive scene Sue had set, it was obvious that something was troubling her. She admitted that what had started as a good relationship with her supervisor had now soured. As a consequence, Sue began to question her decision-making. She said, 'I've literally lost confidence in everything I'm doing at work. I don't know whether my decisions are right or wrong. I'm questioning everything I say and do.'

We asked Sue to tell us about her supervisor. She said they had got on like a house on fire at first, but as Sue became settled and liked by her colleagues and residents, her supervisor became more and more uncooperative. She would point out Sue's faults and called Sue to her office on numerous occasions. She told us she would have digs about most things – even silly little things, such as, 'Mr Brown doesn't like that much milk in his tea', 'Your name badge isn't straight', 'You're too familiar', 'You're too friendly', 'You're unprofessional'. The criticism was relentless, to the point where Sue wondered if she should get another job. But she was worried she would get a bad reference. The constant criticism was affecting her work, her sleep and her happiness, and she just did not know what to do for the best. It was now destroying the things she had loved so much about her new work life. Sue's supervisor was obstructive, cold and critical, and it was clear for us to see that it was breaking this beautiful soul stood in front of us.

We asked Sue a series of questions.

'Who gave you your job?' She said her supervisor and her supervisor's superior, the house manager.

We asked, 'Why did they give you the job?' Sue confirmed that it was because they believed she was competent.

We asked whether both the supervisor and house manager had experience in recruiting. She confirmed that they did, and that both had been in their positions for a long time.

We asked Sue whether the supervisor had started criticising her before or after she had done things that were above and beyond her job description (such as baking treats for residents, and chatting with them and their families, all in her own time). Sue confirmed that it was sometime after.

We asked if Sue's baking and chatting had been warmly received by everyone else. Sue confirmed that they had.

We asked Sue whether she had ever had any official complaints from residents, their families or other work colleagues, or if she'd had any formal disciplinaries? Sue confirmed, 'Never.'

We asked Sue whether her supervisor had ever stayed behind after work, baked, chatted with residents or their families. Sue thought for a moment and said, 'To be fair, no, she's usually already got her coat on before she is due to finish her shift.'

We then asked Sue whether she ever recalled a time at school when she was handing in a piece of work, and then spotted another child's work that appeared magnificent by comparison. We asked Sue how that made her feel back then. Sue laughed and said, 'I would have probably hated that kid, as they were putting my effort to shame.' We asked Sue to now apply that same philosophy to her supervisor. Sue instantly got it as we pointed out that while her supervisor's actions were unpleasant, they were in fact a huge compliment. Sue in every way exceeded her supervisor's work ethic, ability, enthusiasm and popularity.

Sue's realisation that her boss envied her enthusiasm and that she was putting her to shame was evident immediately in her reaction. Sue now felt pity for her supervisor, as she obviously didn't love her job as much as Sue, or maybe had to dash home due to commitments.

We suggested that Sue deal with her manager in a delicate manner, by first giving her compliments if and when she genuinely deserved them, particularly when work related, as it was evident that her supervisor felt threatened by Sue. We suggested Sue say things such as, 'All that paperwork you have to do as a supervisor, I could never do that,' and, 'I have no idea how you manage to get your head around the rotas,' to help alleviate the supervisor's insecurities, which would then make her ease her pressure on Sue. We also suggested that she agree with everything, but then take control, so for example: 'Yes, I see what you're saying, and I love your way of doing it, but I just don't seem to be able to do it that way.' We also suggested that if she said anything hurtful, Sue should reply with: 'I know you probably didn't realise, as I know you are a lovely person, but that comment was really hurtful, so I thought I'd let you know as I'm sure you'd never, ever hurt anyone intentionally.'

We finally suggested that she tell her supervisor, 'I live alone and I get quite lonely, and I know what you said about staying behind after my shift and the baking situation, but because it's good for my mental health and it appears that the residents like it, too, which I know is very important to you, I'm making an appointment to speak to the house manager to see if there's any possible compromise on this situation.'

Sue absolutely loved the ideas we put forward, and said she would update us accordingly, which she kindly did by email some months later:

I went back to work with such a positive attitude, and I felt really good knowing that I was actually really good at my job, which is why my boss was being crabby with me. Anyway, I literally did everything you said, and the difference is like night and day. Things are so much better. Still think I'm not her favourite staff member, but as you said, I know that is a compliment as that's because she's worried that I make her look bad.

Thanks again.

Love Sue.

Boss - a positive perspective

Work colleagues are people who become a significant part of our life, but just like family, they may not be people we would otherwise choose as friends. We will connect with some work colleagues positively, and some we will have to tolerate. It is worth accepting that this is perfectly normal – it would be an unreasonable expectation to try to be best friends with all of our workmates.

Although we do not choose our work colleagues or our superiors, a mutual respect should always exist. No one, not even the person paying your wages, has the right to belittle you, constantly berate you or make you feel bad.

We do have to be understanding that, on rare occasions, in a moment of frustration, stress, misunderstanding or upset, your boss or work colleague might say something hurtful to you. In an otherwise respectful working relationship, this can be accepted as a momentary lapse of judgement, for which one would expect an apology afterwards. We have all had those rare moments ourselves, and therefore we have to understand that even our boss is human. However, if the criticism and hurtful comments are a regular occurrence, rather than a rarity, then the situation must be addressed. It is not acceptable for a colleague or boss to treat you this way; it can and will be incredibly detrimental to your happiness, confidence and self-esteem.

We do understand that you may feel you do not have the confidence to address this, or perhaps you are worried about jeopardising your job. However, there are ways to address a colleague's unacceptable behaviour without confrontation.

Beginning your discussion with a compliment helps to put your work colleague or boss into a positive frame of mind. Trust us, this works whether you believe it or not. As we suggested with our case study, Sue, some great ways to approach the situation would be:

> 'I know that you're a really lovely person, so you won't be doing this on purpose to hurt me, but when you .... it really hurts my feelings. I know you would want to know that, as you wouldn't mean it that way.'

> 'I really respect you, and aspire to be as good as you are, so when you say .... about my work, please could you show me the procedure so I can fully understand and be sure I do it to your satisfaction?'

> 'I may be misunderstanding the situation, and I do hope I am wrong, but I get the feeling you don't like me/the way I do .... so please do let me know what I can do to improve that, as I'd hate to think I was upsetting you.'

> 'I hate to think I could upset you in any way as I really respect you and enjoy working with/for you, but I feel I upset or disappointed you when you said .... and I'd hate for you to feel that way, so do show me what I need/can do to prevent that happening again.'

Often people will vent their frustrations on the person who is least likely to speak out or confront them. So firstly, take comfort from the fact that if your colleague vents on you, it is likely because they think you are a kind person who is probably not going to respond aggressively. However, once you have broached the subject with them, they are less likely to vent on you and, if they do, they are more likely to follow with an apology.

The moment your boss says something unkind or negative, take three or four large sighs to relax your body and address the situation immediately with the words suggested above.

If your boss or superior is not receptive when you raise the issue with them, then this needs to be addressed by approaching someone in a higher position. Again, this can be done without confrontation on the basis of: 'I feel that you may have an issue with me, which saddens me, as I really do like and respect you, but because of that I want to improve the situation, so I think to involve .... as an impartial third party to help would be a great idea.'

Rehearse these lines in advance to boost your confidence and make it easier to stick to your script if you feel nervous.

Finally, do not lose sight of the fact that the negative behaviour of your boss or superior is often due to them feeling inadequate compared to you. They may worry that you are highlighting their failings with your natural abilities. Their actions therefore should be interpreted as a compliment. It may help for them to realise that you have no intention of taking their job, so subtle remarks to reassure them – such as, 'I don't know how you do what you do. I could never cope with the responsibility of .... like you do' – would help.

Do not forget that it is unacceptable to be treated badly or unfairly, especially at work. So you have every right to raise this issue with your boss, and to take it to someone at a higher level if the behaviour continues.

No One Is Born Bad

When we began our journey together as a couple, we realised that our happiness and outlook on life was determined by the schemas (beliefs) we had accumulated through our life experiences and our interpretations. With the understanding that we are all masters of our own destiny, we chose to take responsibility over what guided our beliefs. So we created twelve core schemas to provide us with a better way of looking at the world and a positive foundation for our life ahead together.

1 There is no one reality.

2 Disregard the doubters.

3 Accept responsibility for your life.

4 Anything is possible.

5 Failure only exists when you quit.

6 It's never too late.

7 Plan your life.

8 You are what you eat.

9 Save yourself before you save the world.

10 No one is born bad.

11 You've got to give to receive.

12 You become what you think about.

Having created these schemas, we then practised them daily, until we'd adapted to them as part of our life. Since then these schemas have allowed us to see the world, people and our lives in a far more positive and beneficial way.

While all of the core schemas are important, the one that we feel it is essential to adopt when it comes to boosting confidence is Number 10: 'No one is born bad.' If anyone treats you badly, it's most often because they have been badly treated themselves. If someone has bullied you, it is because they have been bullied or are jealous of you. We hope that knowing and being aware of this will make you realise that anyone who has treated you badly or been unkind to you was doing it out of their own insecurities, rather than because something is wrong with you.

Disregard the Doubters

No matter what you want to do, experience or achieve in your life, there will invariably be people who will feel compelled to cast a shadow on you or your plans with words such as, 'What do you want to do that for?' We call these people 'doubters'. There are generally four reasons why people cast doubt on your plans.

1 The first is envy. The doubter can't be bothered to put the effort in, or is afraid of their own failure, so they can't bear to see you succeed.

2 The doubter applies their knowledge and skills to your plans. Because they doubt themselves and could not consider doing what you have planned, they project their doubts and inabilities on you.

3 The doubter may have a fear of losing you because they may think that bettering yourself will result in you making new friends, meeting new people and potentially moving on with your life and forgetting them.

4 The doubter may be simply unable to relate to your plans. We all want different things in life, so if the doubter can't understand your perspective or motive, they will cast doubt on your idea.

Understanding that those who doubt or question your plans do so out of their own fears and inadequacies will help you to take their comments with a pinch of salt. Everyone has their dreams questioned by others – you have most likely doubted or questioned someone else's plans yourself – but we can learn to trust ourselves more than we trust the feedback of others.

Social Media

We would finally like to touch on social media with you, as this is an area of modern life that has the potential to sabotage, or even destroy, your self-confidence.

There are, of course, many elements of social media that are incredibly positive, such as connecting with friends or finding groups that share your interests. However, social media can be challenging if you are suffering from a lack of confidence and low self-esteem.

Comparison is something that challenges most of us at times on social media: seemingly perfect families, beautiful holiday views, sculpted bodies on display. But we must not lose sight of the fact that people only share their best and most enviable moments. Many pictures are also Photoshopped to the point where you would be unlikely to recognise that same person in real life. It is not worth comparing our own inner struggles with these often fabricated or exaggerated images, which have been carefully curated. In our experience, it is often those with confidence issues and low self-esteem who use social media as a tool to receive attention and appreciation by posting images that present the veneer of a perfect life. When we are truly happy and at peace in life, we don't need the validation of those we only know online.

You are unique, and you will never be satisfied with who you are while you are comparing yourself to someone else. Being kind to yourself is even more important than being kind and honest to others. If you feel vulnerable or upset, it may be a good idea to avoid social media until you are feeling a little more robust.

You may have come across trolls online, who leave vicious comments on posts – either yours or someone else's – and appear to enjoy causing distress. It can be very upsetting to be on the receiving end of these comments, which you would almost never encounter in real life. While it would be very unlikely that someone would approach you in the street to tell you that they hate your hair, or they think you look too fat or thin, it seems that some people have no embarrassment about doing this to someone online. But internet trolls are often people who should be pitied. Their actions are a reflection of their own self-loathing, and they often have no ability to interact in the real world with real people. They compensate for their own issues and emotional pain by punishing others, while hiding behind a keyboard.

We would recommend caution on social media platforms. Immediately block anyone who is unkind and consider unfollowing or muting anyone whose posts you end up using as a comparison to feel unhappy about yourself. This book, and your journey, are all about lifting you up to the light to appreciate the wonderful human being you are, so anything that affects or shadows this possibility should be switched off or blocked.

Actions

Look through your social media platforms and block, silence or unfollow anyone who has a negative impact on you.

Bungee Technique

Having read about confidence saboteurs (see Chapter 5, page 77), for this exercise, we would now like you to identify all potential confidence saboteurs, both in your past and in the present. Look through your timeline and write a list of these people. We would now like to help you emotionally distance yourself or completely sever the negative emotional tie or influence that may exist over you from anyone who has treated you badly in your past or present.

In this and later chapters we speak about confidence saboteurs and draggers and their negative impact and effect on you, your past and your future.

We would now like to share a technique with you that takes away their negative emotional power or influence over you. You will do this with one person at a time from your list. We would also recommend revisiting this technique every time you add or recall someone else who you are adding to your list of saboteurs. Put a big tick at the side of that person and even a smiley face once you have dealt with them to show you have taken control over them.

How it works

We discovered some years ago that everybody has individual coding. What we mean by this is that we all see things and individuals in a certain, often unique, way.

To demonstrate this to you, we would like you to imagine the face of somebody you love unconditionally, someone who is a part of your life; this might be your partner, parent, child or a pet. Now, imagine a picture of their face in front of yours (you may prefer to do this with your eyes closed). Just imagine seeing their face and put your hand where you see and feel their image. Most people will notice that it feels as if that picture of their loved one's face is in front of them, very close to their face, maybe slightly to the left or slightly to the right, but it is generally quite close up. Therefore, put your hand where you see or feel the image. Notice where your hand is, and in particular the position.

Try this again, but think about another person you really care about, who you love or who is a part of your life. Close your eyes if you prefer, but imagine their face – again, put your hand where you see or feel it. Again, you will notice that it feels as though their picture is close to you, perhaps in the same place, or slightly to the left or right, or above or below the previous person you tried this with.

Now we would like you to try this with a person you haven't seen for a very long time, somebody who isn't that important to you, maybe somebody you once went to school with, or even an old school teacher – but your feelings towards them are indifferent. You should notice that, this time, this less important person's image is much further away from you and perhaps not as clear.

Having carried out this exercise, it should be clear that your coding positions people who are important to you close to you, whereas those who are less significant in your life are further away.

We would now like to establish your coding of the saboteurs, bullies and draggers you have experienced in your life, and where you see the position of their face. If their actions and words still affect you, your behaviours, your confidence, self-esteem and self-worth, then you may be surprised to notice that you see their image very close to your face. This is based on your unconscious coding.

The fact that you have coded them so close to you highlights that their actions have continued to overshadow your daily life.

If you would now like to sever that emotional tie from the past so that they and their actions no longer have any power over you, and you are ready to take control, we would now like you to move their image very far into the distance.

You can do this with your eyes open (or close them if it is easier for you). Imagine this negative person's image, which is likely to be close to you, being attached to a tight bungee cord.

You then need to imagine yourself cutting the cord and releasing them, watching their image fly into the distance, getting smaller and smaller, further and further away until they disappear.

You will repeat this four or five times, seeing yourself cutting that bungee cord and allowing them to fly far into the distance until they disappear.

On the final time you do this, when the image of the person disappears into the distance close your eyes and sigh three or four times (ensure that those sighs are big sighs), knowing that their image has disappeared and their impact on you has been demolished forever.

Now when you think about the negative person you should notice that their image is difficult to find, far away or you just don't see it at all. You should now have a neutral feeling about them, and you should notice that you feel stronger and more in control.

It's no exaggeration to say that the Speakmans' workshop event yesterday was truly life-changing! I can't even begin to thank the Speakmans enough . . . you are exceptional!!!
Becca

Increasing self-worth with the Bungee Technique

Just as you imagined the people who had wronged you and moved their image further away, we now want you to find your own image and bring it closer, so you can regain or take control of yourself and your life with confidence.

Where do you see yourself? Where is your image? You may find this a little more challenging, but look high and low, near and far, or are you even behind you?

Whereas before you cut the bungee cord, this time, with your eyes closed, use it to pull your picture close to you, near to your face, perhaps even to just above your forehead. Imagine that image of you close, clear, strong and confident. Make that picture larger and then sigh three or four times, ensuring they are big sighs. After doing this a few times you should find you have a stronger image of yourself, and stronger confidence with it.

I've changed so much . . . I'm off my meds . . . I've gone back to work . . . I love me again. I'm going to a concert by myself as I now can.

Thank you.

Vanessa

6

The Worst That Can Happen

I arrived very low, in a difficult place in my life, but left in a much better place and have been in a better place ever since. My wife has commented many times [that] I am like a different person and can see I am trying and working on ways to handle my circumstances in a more positive way. From the bottom of my heart, thank you for everything.

Kay

What Stops Us?

Undoubtedly, the most significant barrier to you speaking out or stepping out of your comfort zone is your negative schema that presents you with all the potential catastrophes that could occur. Fear of what might happen becomes bigger than the desire to change. This fear acts like an invisible roadblock, stopping you from getting to your desired destination.

Your brain cannot tell the difference between something that has happened and something that you have vividly imagined.

As you consider all the possible negative outcomes of taking the steps you want to take, you will often feel physical discomfort, as if the very worst is actually happening. Your heart may beat faster and you may begin to breathe more shallowly just imagining everything that might happen. There is a physiological reason for this: your imagined worst-case scenario feels real and so stress hormones are released. These hormones shut down your reflective function, which allows us to distinguish between imagination and perception. In the most basic terms, this means your body acts as if your fabricated worst-case scenario is actually happening. We have found, in treating countless individuals, that the worst-case scenario happens rarely and even when it does, the fallout is usually significantly less traumatic than expected.

The truth is that you are not a fortune teller. Your imagined future is just something you have made up; it's not a prediction of what will happen. This is great news, as you can have the peace of mind that comes from knowing you have absolutely no ability to predict situations, people's thoughts or reactions.

There Is No One Reality

No one will see the world quite like you. No one will have the exact same values, beliefs or opinions as anyone else because everyone has different life experiences. You may think people will not like you, what you do or what you say, or that they may react to you in a certain way, but this is impossible for you to predict. So try to let go of imagining all the possible things that might go wrong. Furthermore, everyone's opinion is based upon their own personal schemas, so you and a friend will often perceive the same situation in very different ways.

Nothing highlights this more than the legal system, where two opposing parties can pay millions of pounds in legal fees defending their position as they both insist they are right. They say there are two sides to every story, but in actuality there are three: each party's perspective of a situation and the absolute truth. You see, we don't believe what we see, we see what we already believe! This is why you may do an outstanding piece of work, but if you already have the belief that your efforts are never good enough then you will not allow yourself to see how incredible the work is or, even more so, how incredible you really are, too.

As with all situations in life, it's important to look at things from more than one angle. We instinctively apply our view of the world, our life skills and our knowledge to every situation we encounter, and immediately make an assumption based on our personal experiences. Yet often we can be so wrong. For example, you might have experienced the situation when you have not heard from a friend for a while and you start wondering if perhaps you've upset them. You start mentally going through all of your interactions with your friend, looking for what you might have done wrong. Then your friend calls to say that their mobile phone was broken and they've been waiting for a replacement. You may have spent days worrying unnecessarily, because you had forgotten that it is impossible to mind-read other people's thoughts or feelings.

> **'There is nothing either good or bad, but thinking makes it so.'**
> **William Shakespeare, *Hamlet***

The Worst-case Scenarios

Negative schemas, and negative past life events, create negative thought processes. As a consequence, the worst-case scenarios you might dwell upon and fear could include:

Judgement

Rejection

Humiliation/Ridicule

Blushing (see Chapter 8, Shyness and Blushing, page 187)

Carrying out the Bungee Technique in Chapter 5 (see page 124) on yourself to inflate your self-worth will make these fears less relevant to you. Also, addressing and understanding these topics will help reduce their power over you, and help you to push past your emotional roadblocks.

Judgement

The majority of us want to be liked. As a consequence, we are sensitive to how others perceive us, and most of us do our utmost to interact with others cordially.

However, if you are suffering with low self-esteem or a lack of confidence, if you have been bullied, abused or humiliated, this understandably leads to insecurities. These insecurities make you hypersensitive to what others may think, feel or say about you.

Your fear of judgement can stop you:

* **Sharing your ideas**

* **Telling people how you feel**

* **Saying I love you**

* Asking for a promotion or raise

* Speaking out about your choice

* Choosing what film to watch

* Deciding which restaurant to go to

* Asking someone on a date

* Speaking up about an injustice to you or others

* Public speaking

* Being a best man/bridesmaid/maid of honour/usher

* Raising a dissatisfaction of any kind

* Stepping outside your front door

A fear of judgement in most cases is a reflection of our own insecurities. Your anticipation of judgement is based on you expecting to fail or humiliate yourself.

But as we have established, you are not a mind reader. You cannot know what others are thinking or feeling. So your fear of someone judging you is actually based on you judging yourself. This is something you should think about for a few moments, as you may have spent a long time considering the perceived judgements of others without questioning your internal judgement. Please trust us when we say that you are a kind person, you are understanding and sympathetic. You have good values. Therefore an unkind judgement, whether that be of yourself or others, is not in your nature. With this knowledge you can now challenge yourself, reminding yourself of this whenever your habitual behaviours of self-judgement arise: *I am a kind person with good values, and harsh judgement is not in my nature.*

Your past life experiences, and the actions of others in your past, may have made you learn to expect, and consequently fear, judgement. Yet our schemas mean that we take the reins of judgement ourselves, anticipating it and judging ourselves on behalf of others based on what they may or may not have thought about us in the past.

> *Judging yourself is like taking over where the bully, judgemental parent, friend or ex-partner left off.*

We hope that reading this book, understanding the processes and completing the exercises will help you learn to trust, love, respect and believe in yourself, so as not to be consumed by the worry of others judging you negatively.

Addressing your fear of being judged

1 Change your perception

Your perception of judgement thus far may have been negative. However, we all judge, most of the time. You make a cup of tea and judge whether it is to your satisfaction. You judge if it has been brewed long enough, whether it's sweet enough, too hot or too cold. This is judgement.

You eat a meal; you judge how it tastes. You watch a movie; you judge whether you enjoy it. You get into bed; you judge whether you are in a comfortable position.

Judgement is communication, progression and also, importantly, an education. Judgement allows us to choose things we like and dislike. As we obtain new information, we can judge it, assess it and move forward.

Judgement is a tool, that is all. It is not necessarily negative.

You may, up to this point, have judged 'judgement' unfairly due to your past experiences. You may have seen it as negative, but we would now like you to see judgement as a positive, and be able to recognise all the benefits it can bring you. You would not have the qualifications you have if your work had not been judged. You would not be able to drive had your driving skills not been judged. You would not be in the job you are in had you not been judged as the best candidate. You would not have the partner or friends you have had they not judged you as someone they wanted in their life.

2 Be kind

You may question the relevance of suggesting kindness when addressing a fear of judgement. Please consider that when you fear someone is judging you harshly, you are being unkind not only to yourself, but also to the other person or people by assuming that their thoughts are harsh and negative. This is quite an insulting thing to project onto someone who may be incredibly kind and lovely.

We suggest that with every negative judgement you fabricate, you stop for a moment and think, 'Be kind.' Consider:

It is unfair to accuse someone of judging me negatively because of .... [name of person who made you feel bad] from my past.

It is unfair to assume that people want to judge me with criticism.

It is disrespectful to be unkind to anyone, including myself.

Impartial fair judgement is how I grow and learn.

Judgement helps me to make a choice.

If any or all of these statements resonate with you, it is a great idea to write them on the front of your diary, make them a screen saver or write them on an index card to keep in your purse, on your bedroom mirror or on the sun visor in your car. Put the reminder somewhere you can see it daily, to reinforce the message that judgement is a tool, not a negative criticism.

3 See it for what it was and not how it felt

An event or events contributed to you feeling judged or being sensitive to judgement. Look at your timeline and begin to investigate and understand the events that started your hyperawareness to judgement.

Consider the situation again so as to work out what actually happened, as opposed to how it felt in the moment. The benefit of hindsight and adult wisdom can help us reframe these moments when we first built the schema of judgement.

For example:

If a parent or family member was judgemental . . .

Was this an act of love in an effort to make you the best possible version of yourself? Was this their way of showing that they cared about you and wanted you to be perfect? Was the judgement because they made mistakes, and they were trying to shield you from making the same mistakes as them? Was it because they considered themselves an underachiever, or because they were trying to enjoy success in their life through your achievements? Were they envious of you? Did they feel lesser than you so were trying to pull you down to feel better about themselves?

If a teacher was judgemental . . .

Was this their effort to encourage you? Did they misunderstand your efforts? Were they quite cantankerous to everyone, so their judgement was not personal to you?

If a partner was judgemental . . .

Were they having a bad day? Were they scared of losing you so were extra critical to try to make you feel grateful for their love? Did they think you were too good for them, so were trying to pull you down to inflate their status?

If a work colleague, friend or sibling was judgemental . . .

Were they envious of you? Were you putting them to shame and they were jealous? Were they trying to justify their position? Did they misunderstand? Were they having personal issues that made them irritable?

4 Communication

The best way to obtain solid evidence that your assumptions and accusations of negativity from a third party are entirely inaccurate is to ask people for feedback. To accuse is insulting, but to ask for feedback on anything is a compliment to the person you're asking, as it highlights that you respect them and their knowledge and appreciate their opinion.

5 Do they matter?

Before you stop yourself from doing something due to worry about judgement and what people think of you, do consider first, do they really matter? So what if they don't approve?

Someone else's standards may be different to yours and that is OK. Their judgement is based upon their own standards and abilities, which are not likely to match yours.

If your fear of judgement started due to someone from the past, ask yourself if they still matter. Why are you frantically still trying to impress someone who may no longer be a part of your life?

There is only one person who will be with you twenty-four hours a day, seven days a week, for the rest of your life. That person is you, and therefore only *you* matter. Your own standard is good enough. Your best is good enough. Most of all, *you* are good enough.

Rejection

For those with low self-esteem, fear of rejection can lead to compromising yourself and your values just so that you can please others. This creation of a false self that we feel is more palatable than our real self can fuel still more insecurities.

We are also more eager to please and to tolerate unacceptable behaviour so that we can avoid rejection. However, this behaviour can make you seem needy and insecure, which could in itself lead to rejection.

Your attempts to please in order to avoid rejection can make you more susceptible to becoming a victim of abuse, bullying or general manipulation. Furthermore, your fear of rejection can prevent you from experiencing the job you really want, the person you really want to date and the loving and respectful friends and relationships you deserve.

> *Rejection offers resistance. Resistance promotes growth.*

CASE STUDY
Julie: Fear of Rejection

Julie attended our clinic after trying numerous therapies, medications and an abundance of natural treatments to remedy her fear of rejection. She had been given numerous diagnoses, including depression, generalised anxiety disorder and borderline personality disorder. Her thoughts were consumed with the fact that her partner would have an affair and leave her, her children would choose their father over her, her friends would realise she was not the person they thought and leave her, and she would be left alone.

We learned from Julie's questionnaires that she was the youngest of three children, and came from a loving home with doting parents. Despite this, her timeline told the story of a number of failed relationships and events that she classed as failures, such as hanging out with the wrong crowd at school and choosing the wrong partners.

Although a proud mum of two, Julie described herself as overprotective and intense.

The patterns in Julie's life consistently repeated. She would make friends or date someone, and then her overeagerness to please would make her intense. She would then feel bitter that she was giving so much and obtaining so little in return. Relationships would sour and break, leaving Julie devastated.

Julie's biggest fear was her children leaving for university, which was imminent. In her words, the idea had made her 'physically sick and have panic attacks'. This led to the thought of her partner being totally fed up with her neediness and leaving her for someone else, to which she added: 'And I wouldn't blame him.'

It was evident that Julie was doing everything to prevent rejection, yet her positive intentions and actions were actually destroying the relationships she was so desperate to keep.

When we asked Julie where she felt this pattern of behaviour had started, she assumed it was when she had made her very first friend at junior school and their friendship had broken apart. However, on further questioning, Julie revealed that even then she had been incredibly eager to please and thus this was actually a consequence of her fear-of-rejection 'schema', which was already in place.

We were stumped. There was no obvious moment in Julie's past that had caused her destructive behaviours, but at least we now had evidence that this behaviour had started prior to the break-up of her friendship at junior school. Julie's early years appeared idyllic; her parents were attentive, she got on with her sisters, yet Julie had a definite issue and a hyperawareness towards rejection from a young age.

To help us try to understand the potential origin further, we asked Julie to tell us more about her family. It was then that

Julie gave us the missing piece of information that provided us with our eureka moment, enabling us to condition her destructive schemas.

Julie was the youngest of three girls. By the time she was born, both her sisters were already at school. Her sisters shared a bedroom, whereas Julie had a small box room to herself, and she remembers that if ever she felt scared in the night, she would often go into her sisters' room, and equally often would be told to go back to her own.

It was then that we posed a question to Julie. We asked: 'As a little girl, your sisters were sharing a room, your parents were sharing a room, but you were the odd one out, all alone. How did that make you feel?'

Julie suddenly became visibly upset and began to cry. There was an immediate change in her body language. She rounded her shoulders, brought her arms and knees together and adopted a childlike pose. It was evident we had hit a nerve.

After a few moments, Julie told us that she had not ever thought about that, but looking back she always felt lonely. This realisation had a significantly profound impact on Julie. She was stunned but relieved to have an explanation for her lifetime of ruinous behaviour. She said, 'I honestly thought I was broken and made all this up – this is such a relief and an eye-opener.' Julie had resigned herself to the belief that she was destined for a life of unhappiness, as she must have been born this way, yet she now had an explanation that felt right to her, and for the first time in many years she also had hope of a brighter future.

We asked Julie whether she shared a room with her partner. Julie responded that she did. We asked whether this meant she favoured her partner over her children. Julie responded, 'Of course not.' She accepted that her parents sharing a bedroom was right and bore no reflection on her. We said, 'Are you sure, then, that when you were born your parents did not sit together with you as their new baby and have the discussion, so who's going to share with who?' Julie giggled and said, 'Of course not.'

We then moved on to her sisters, and asked, 'Why do you think your sisters shared a bedroom?' Julie confirmed that it was because she was the last one to be born, but she also added, 'But I was the youngest, so I should've shared and my oldest sister should have had the box room.'

The truth was obvious to us, and now we had to help Julie see the likely explanation. We asked: 'So your sisters were already at school when you were born?' Julie confirmed that they were. We went on, 'And your sisters had to be up for school, and you didn't?' Julie again confirmed that was correct.

'Did your sisters go to bed later than you because they were older?' Julie said, 'Most likely, yes.'

We concluded: 'Julie, can we ask you, as a mum, when you had your children and they were toddlers and they had just fallen asleep, how would you behave once they'd fallen asleep if you had to go to the toilet or to bed yourself?'

Julie confirmed that she would try to be as quiet as possible so as not to disturb her children.

We asked again: 'Julie, in view of what we have just discussed, why do you think your parents put your sisters together in the same bedroom and put you on your own? Was it just to upset you? To ostracise you?'

Julie looked at us and said, 'Wow. I totally got that wrong, didn't I?'

Pointing out that her parents had given her a room on her own so that her sisters did not disturb her had lifted a very heavy weight and entirely restructured what had been a very negative schema. Julie completely accepted that she had never been rejected and, on the contrary, was very much loved.

Reject rejection

If you have an extreme fear of rejection, it is likely that, like Julie's story, this will be a consequence of:

* **A past event that needs to be addressed positively**
* **A misunderstanding**
* **Low self-esteem**
* **Lack of confidence**
* **Loneliness**
* **A need for love**
* **A need for belonging**

Understanding your behaviour will allow you to address it more effectively. So we would like you to take another look at your timeline to consider your life events from a new perspective. Just as we did with Julie, look for clues to events you may have interpreted as rejection.

These events need to be challenged by your present self, and we offer suggestions on how to challenge your inaccurate negative schemas at the end of this chapter (see page 155). However, in order to understand what really happened, try and consider:

Had you perhaps misunderstood the situation?

Was that break-up a blessing?

Did that person even deserve you?

Did you learn something positive from that experience?

Did that relationship teach you something?

Was someone's behaviour personal to you or a symptom of their own issues?

Did rejection lead you to something better?

Was it rejection, or just growing in different directions?

Was it just circumstance?

Remember, there is only one person who will be with you every moment, every day and always: that is you, and you have assurance and certainty in this. Others will come and go. Some friendships or relationships will last only minutes, such as the person you're chatting to while waiting to see your dentist, for example. Some will last hours, such as the passenger sitting at your side on an aircraft. Some will last only days, like the colleague you meet on a course. Some will last for weeks, others for months and some for years. People have and will come in and out of your life. Their departure is not a rejection; they are just moving on, as you will be, too.

We would like you to consider an analogy we often use, which is that relationships are just like shoes.

Some will look amazing but hurt your feet when you walk.

Some will give you blisters.

Some will not match every outfit.

Some will not match every occasion.

Some are just your favourites.

Some fit snugly.

Some will fall apart after a few wears.

Some, with the odd repair, or occasional reheel, can last you a lifetime.

However, your feet are perfect the way they are, and having a cupboard full of shoes is not essential.

Shoes do not give you blisters to spite you; they simply don't fit right. They don't break to punish you or because of you; they just wear out over time.

I wanted to let you know what incredible changes are happening and how grateful I am. My life has already inexplicably changed forever.

My self-esteem was my biggest issue and I was self-sabotaging relationships with loved ones because of it.

All the past negative beliefs have fallen apart and no longer make sense to me. I am so thankful. I feel like I have new eyes and am now following my dreams with those I love.

My eternal thanks.

Rosa

Humiliation/Ridicule

When we refer to humiliation or ridicule in association with lack of confidence, we are primarily looking at events that, when you consider them, are associated with a feeling of embarrassment. Perhaps you made a mistake, said or did something that made people laugh or stare. We have all experienced situations when we felt we had humiliated ourselves or been ridiculed.

How we are perceived by others is a driver in our avoidance of doing, saying or instigating anything that may make us stand out as a target for laughter, humiliation or ridicule.

If we trip up and stumble over our feet when we are in private or at home, we dust ourselves down and carry on. But if we stumble and fall while we are out in public, often our first response is not 'Have I hurt myself?' but 'Did anyone see me?'

Being humiliated or ridiculed creates embarrassment and this is an emotion we try to avoid at all costs, as it simply feels too uncomfortable. This discomfort triggers our internal protection mechanism, releasing adrenaline and resulting in all the symptoms that we label as anxiety. This includes a fast-beating heart, mouth dryness, feeling hot and being breathless.

If your avoidance of social situations, public speaking or generally standing out is extreme, it is possible that you may be suffering with social anxiety or glossophobia (a fear of public speaking – see Chapter 7, page 159).

Overzealous efforts to avoid humiliation and ridicule can prevent people from stepping out of their comfort zone, and it can hold us back from sharing ourselves, our qualities and our skills. So many of the people we meet at our clinic and workshops who suffer from low confidence are held back by worry over the repercussions of standing out, being laughed at, humiliated or ridiculed.

Reducing the power of humiliation

If you refuse to attempt tasks due to the worry of being humiliated, then we are here to help. Our approach is to positively challenge your interpretation of any negative past life events that contribute to your heightened awareness associated with humiliation.

If you can recall a situation in which you were humiliated or embarrassed, then let's look more closely at what happened. On this occasion, rather than recalling exactly as it felt at the time, it is important to be an outside observer of that memory and not in the lead role. After seeing the memory in your mind's eye, now imagine watching that memory as a short film on a television screen. This technique allows you to see the situation without the emotional attachments. So now consider what actually went wrong. While it may have felt uncomfortable at the time, now that you see it as an observer, what actually happened?

If this was an incident from school, consider how many of your school friends may have done something to embarrass themselves, and how many of those moments you actually remember. In the unlikely event that you do remember any occasions, consider how you feel about the person who was embarrassed or humiliated. Do you think any less of them or do you actually feel for them more, due to what they went through?

The truth is that most people will feel understanding and sympathy for anyone who has had a fall or said or done something by mistake or accident. Consider that those moments you describe as humiliating, someone else may describe as endearing.

We would also like you to consider an alternative perspective on your avoidance of humiliation and exposure. Have you ever thought that hiding yourself away from the world is a selfish act? You are preventing people from benefiting from your friendship, your love, your wisdom, your opinions and your contribution to this world.

When the Worst Was Expected

You have no doubt experienced situations that you expected to be horrific or catastrophic, yet you came out the other side with gratitude and improved confidence. That could be going to a party you dreaded that turned out to be fun, where you caught up with or made new friends. That talk you were forced to give at school, that actually worked out well and won you praise and compliments. That difficult issue you really did not want to address, that cleared the air and made your relationship much stronger.

Consider these events and add them to the positive list on your timeline before you read on further. Don't forget, your timeline can be numerous pages, and the more positive events you add and consider, the more beneficial this will be to building your confidence.

If you are doubting us right now, let us remind you that for many well-known people their worst expectation proved to be the most wonderfully positive act of their life. The truth is that being open and honest, and being yourself, will allow you to thrive. When you allow yourself to be the person you were born to be, and should have been, you then find that inner confidence you most likely did not even know existed.

Some incredibly inspirational examples are:

GARETH THOMAS

Gareth Thomas was the first man in professional rugby union to openly admit he was gay. He battled with his sexuality, believing he would be rejected because of it, and married his childhood sweetheart in an attempt to deny his truth. He concocted a whole host of worst-case scenarios about coming out, expecting them all to be catastrophic, ending his career, his friendships and also the respect he had gained over the years and worked so hard for. But after hiding a big secret left him feeling so low that he contemplated suicide, he told his teammates. To Gareth's surprise they were incredibly supportive and kept his secret for three years until he decided to open up publicly.

When he did speak up publicly, he proved to himself that the worst-case scenario fabrications of his own inner critic were entirely wrong. He gained the love and respect of the country for his bravery, and opened a door for others to talk openly about their sexuality, too.

CAITLYN JENNER

Bruce Jenner was born in New York in 1949 and knew from a young age that he had thoughts and feelings that back then had not even been given a name and certainly were not spoken about. In an interview, Caitlyn shared that as a child, she was fascinated with her older sister's clothes, and said that when she looked in the mirror, she hated what she saw.

Caitlyn did not know how to give a name to her experiences, uncertain if she was a cross-dresser or gay. None of the labels she found felt right.

To distract from the internal conflict, Caitlyn – then known as Bruce – embraced athletics as a distraction from the inner turmoil and confusion.

Caitlyn tried to transition in the 1980s but, too fearful of the consequences, hid who she was supposed to be. However, after decades of hiding due to the possible consequences of potential 'worst-case scenarios', the world finally met the very beautiful and brave Caitlyn, at the age of sixty-nine, and she has inspired so many.

Caitlyn has spoken about how simple her life is now that she gets to be fully herself.

MATTHEW PERRY

Friends star Matthew Perry, who played Chandler Bing throughout the ten incredibly successful years of the show, has admitted that he struggles to recall around three years of his life at the peak of his success, due to serious addiction issues.

Matthew tried to hide his problem from himself and others, and was in denial for years. However, after finally being honest with himself, he checked into rehab.

On his return to the show, instead of the worst-case scenarios he had imagined, such as everyone turning against him or even the possibility of losing his career, Matthew was welcomed back with open arms and with the show's executive producer saying, 'I'm so happy you're back.'

Thanks to this dark and low period in his life, Matthew has gone on to help others who have struggled with addiction. Instead of being judged negatively, he has now become a spokesperson for addiction and drug rehabilitation. He has also been honoured at the White House for his work promoting drug recovery, receiving a Champion of Recovery award.

> *Thanks to our schemas, we don't believe what we see, we see what we already believe.*

When the Worst HAS Happened

Can you imagine the worst actually happening, and in front of thousands people, even the entire world? It is essential to put things into perspective and appreciate that, even when the very worst happens, it really is not that bad.

DAVID HASSELHOFF

David Hasselhoff is an American actor, singer, producer and businessman who once set a Guinness World Record as the most watched man on television.

However, the *Knight Rider* and *Baywatch* actor was shamed by his sixteen-year-old daughter when she videoed him in an intoxicated state as he lay on the floor, half-naked and ranting incoherently while eating a burger off the floor. His daughter could be heard begging him to stop drinking. Footage from the video was leaked in 2007.

This worst-case scenario did not destroy David but helped him to take action to get well. Today he is sober, he goes to AA meetings, he has married again and has a good relationship with his daughters, perhaps directly as a result of facing worldwide humiliation. His career, too, improved as he went on to judge *America's Got Talent* and *Britain's Got Talent*, hosted his own talk show and won roles in movies, pantomime and theatre productions.

ZAC EFRON

Actor and singer Zac Efron shot to fame in the *High School Musical* teen movies. He was a clean-cut, wholesome Disney star when he accidentally dropped a condom on the red carpet at the premiere of a children's movie, to his obvious embarrassment. However, the reaction from the media was pretty generous, with many journalists relating to his mortified I-can't-believe-that-just-happened expression.

Zac is a great example of how feeling embarrassed, and showing it, is a great sign that you are humble, can be apologetic and, most of all, really care. The incident certainly didn't damage his career, which has gone from strength to strength.

FERGIE DUHAMEL

To wet your pants, even in front of your very best friend, could feel uncomfortable, so imagine wetting your pants on stage in front of thousands of people and that footage then going viral around the world.

Fergie, the lead singer of the Black Eyed Peas, was stuck in Friday-night rush-hour traffic on the way to perform in San Diego, California. She was desperate to use the bathroom, but the band arrived so late that they were rushed on to the stage without the chance to use the toilet facilities. She wet her pants on stage, and the incident was photographed and spread all around the world.

Although of course incredibly embarrassing, this incident did not at all damage Fergie's career or reputation. Instead, this faux pas resulted in supportive headlines such as 'Fergie Was a Hero for Peeing Her Pants on Stage'.

These examples show that even when the worst DOES happen, the results are rarely as bad as you may imagine.

Making the Worst the Best

Within moments you completely turned around my thinking. I am not, and was never, at fault. Thank you so much.

Melanie

Overthinking can be your worst enemy as invariably it leads to catastrophising the outcome of anything you are considering. If you are thinking of leaving your job, for example, you may imagine that you will never find another job again, and end up losing your home and family all because of that one wrong decision. If you decide you want to do something, try to consider instead how it may go your way, and how that would feel. How could this action you are contemplating benefit you, and how could it benefit others?

When you feel yourself catastrophising, catch yourself in the moment and challenge it. Ask yourself if you are a fortune teller with the ability to predict the future. Remind yourself that the worst-case scenario may not happen, and good things may result from your actions. When you challenge and distract your overthinking, you will notice that you feel calmer and also less self-conscious.

It is also wise to be cautious about asking for advice from negative people, as they can only apply their own limited thinking to any of your ideas. If they believe they are incapable of doing something, they will advise you against your plans.

To build your confidence and prevent catastrophic thinking, remind yourself of the things you have achieved in your life, and of the times when things have gone well. Keep reading over the positives on your timeline and keep adding any achievements to your positive list. Do not underestimate or be dismissive of the positives in your life. The kindnesses you have shown, the compliments and thanks you have received, the tasks you have completed, the smiles and laughter you have given and shared. These are all achievements and you should remind yourself of them often. We are socially conditioned not to blow our own trumpet – we're told this is bragging or gloating or showing off. While we understand the theory behind that, when it comes to confidence, you have to celebrate your success and achievements to spur you on to achieve more. So it's time to find that dusty trumpet, clean it down and start blowing it!

Look through your timeline, identifying positive scenarios and newly positive interpretations of events you had previously noted as negative. The event may have been negative, but something positive will have come from it, even if it's resilience, empathy, wisdom or the ability to offer help to someone else as a consequence of what you have been through. You cannot change the past, but you can certainly change your perception of it, and find strength in the fact that whatever happened is now over.

Re-examine anything on your timeline and in your questionnaire that you noted as a failure. Failure only exists when you quit, and the fact that you are reading this book and looking to feel stronger, happier and more confident shows that you are far from a quitter. Also consider failure as an opportunity to learn how to improve, or even a lesson in how not to do something.

> 'Failure is important . . . We learn by failure.'
> **James Dyson**[14]

When James Dyson invented his first Dual Cyclone vacuum cleaner, he spent fifteen years creating 5,126 versions that failed before he made one that worked. It took over five thousand failures to create his success. Imagine if he had given up at version 5,125!

If you appreciate your failures and mistakes as the valuable lessons that they are, this will allow you to build your confidence, applaud your efforts and blow your own trumpet.

Thinking the worst is a learned behaviour that becomes habitual. Addressing the schema, or learning, that created the behaviour, together with creating new habits, will restructure and retrain your thinking. To do this, the moment you imagine a worst-case scenario add 'but possibly . . .' and offer yourself a new, more positive possibility to consider.

For example: *If I leave my job, I may end up losing my home and my family and regretting it forever. But possibly I will find a wonderful new job that pays more yet allows me to spend more time with my family.*

Although this is something that you will have to do consciously to start with, and while you may not even believe the positive words at first, the good news is that you will be creating new habits. New, more positive habits will create new, more positive feelings and outcomes. Initially this will take conscious effort, but eventually it will become an unconscious habit that makes you feel effortlessly confident.

Challenging Your Negative Schemas and Behaviours

Return to your self-esteem questionnaire and your timeline (see pages 46 and 18).

Challenging your schemas and coming up with positive evidence to combat them is individual to your own personal circumstances and to each event. However, to help, here are some suggestions of questions you may be able to apply to positively condition a life-hindering schema from your past.

Was it personal to you?

Asking this question is a significant element in our work when helping someone, as often the feeling that you were targeted specifically for being you is detrimental to your confidence and traps you as a victim indefinitely.

It is therefore important to look for evidence as to why it was not personal. For example, we helped a lady who was randomly attacked. She had been blaming herself for the attack. When we helped her to realise – and she accepted – that her attacker had been waiting for a female victim, but not specifically for her, she was freed from this burden.

Similarly, in a violent relationship, although the abuse may feel personal, the fact is that your partner wasn't aggressive only with and specifically because of you – they were aggressive with a partner, any partner and all partners. They will have been aggressive with partners before you, and will be with partners after you, too, because they have aggression issues. This also applies to being bullied. Bullies are not aiming to hurt you personally, but rather to give themselves a sense of power to counteract their own feelings of inadequacy.

Accepting that your trauma was not personal to you negates the belief that you are a target, or that you deserved it in any way.

Copying a parent

If you have a parent who lacked confidence, and you have copied their behaviour, then you must consider that you have no reason to lack confidence. The behaviour does not belong to you; it belonged to your parent. Ask yourself: 'Did lacking confidence enhance my parent's life? If not, why not?' When you catch yourself feeling scared and lacking in confidence, remind yourself: 'I am fine – this isn't me, it's my parent, and I am NOT my parent.'

Criticism

If you were criticised – for example, by a teacher, ex-boss or ex-partner – challenge your belief by asking yourself: 'Do I still want to be listening to this person? What skills did they have that gave them the right to judge me in the first place? And if they were kind people, they wouldn't have judged me, so I shouldn't be listening to them.'

A turbulent past

If there was a time in your life when a series of things went wrong, you may have created an expectation that things will go wrong in the future, causing you to lose confidence in trying, doing, experiencing or experimenting with new things.

Look at the evidence and challenge it. Consider or write down the many things that have gone right in your life. For example, deciding to go somewhere and getting there, passing an exam, making a best friend, having a loving family, buying a home, having children, winning tickets to a concert, baking a cake, cooking a great dinner, getting a bargain or going on holiday. If you keep a diary, document one great thing that happened in your day before bed every night. This will start to retrain your thought patterns and create new positive behavioural habits.

Realistically, there will probably be too many things in your life that have gone right to remember, and only a handful of things that have gone wrong.

I am writing to say a heartfelt thank you. I left feeling a different man. It isn't very often we have a day in our lives that has such a huge impact. Nik and Eva have given me a tremendous springboard of personal growth.

Dave

7

Social Anxiety, Glossophobia and Speaking Out

In just a few minutes, you were able to get me to see things very differently. Thank you for that.

Best wishes x

Linda

In this chapter we want to help you address social anxiety, the fear associated with public speaking and speaking out generally in everyday life. We hope that you can read the case studies and suggestions we share and imagine we are speaking to you directly, to enable you to make the necessary positive changes.

Your voice is a gift. It has the power to create peace with discussion and understanding. When you use your words wisely you can create empathy and inspiration. It can educate through sharing. It can create happiness and security with the words 'I love you'. It can bring laughter to a saddened soul, friendship through chatter, forgiveness with 'I'm sorry' and so, so much more.

Your voice is your power, and it is all yours, to be taken advantage of to create your happiness. You should therefore embrace and use what is rightfully yours frequently and confidently. You may not feel it is possible right now, and you may feel that you have been silenced by others. We want to help you regain your voice.

Your biggest asset is knowing that you have a voice, and the ability to use it.

So many of us look at people in the public eye, even our friends and family who we may look upon with awe, and wonder, 'How do they do it?' We assume that everyone else is comfortable to speak out with confidence, but the truth is, according to the National Institute of Mental Health, that 73 per cent of the US population are affected by social anxiety or a fear of public speaking (also known as glossophobia).[15]

Be assured, if you feel hesitant about speaking in public, you are not alone. In fact, you are in the majority. Many famous people have spoken about their own issues with fear of public speaking, including Richard Branson, Nicole Kidman and Tiger Woods. Just because we see someone speaking confidently in public, it does not mean that they feel confident in that situation – they may just be very good at disguising their anxiety in the moment. So please don't tell yourself that your fear is a sign that you should stay quiet.

What Is Social Anxiety?

Social anxiety, previously known as 'social phobia', affects millions of people all over the world. It is a fear of any social situation involving interaction with other people and, more pertinently, the anxiety of being negatively judged and evaluated by those people. It can be a debilitating disorder that impedes everyday tasks, such as presentations at work or university, giving a team talk to a group of colleagues or simple activities that the majority of the population take for granted, like socialising with friends or interacting with a shop assistant.

According to the US Social Anxiety Institute, social anxiety disorder is the third largest psychological disorder in the country after depression and alcoholism.[16]

For those who suffer from social anxiety, there are many triggers, and while some triggers may be unique to the individual, some of the most common are:

* **Meeting new people**
* **Public speaking**
* **Random small talk**
* **Speaking to people in authority**
* **Speaking up in a meeting**
* **Speaking out on a course/in a classroom scenario**
* **Doing a speech**
* **Going on a date**
* **Performing on stage**
* **Being watched performing a task**
* **Being teased**
* **Being the centre of attention**
* **Speaking on the phone**
* **Being a spokesperson for a group**
* **Being criticised**
* **Returning an unsatisfactory meal in a restaurant**

For people with social anxiety, their fear is often of being the centre of attention, being judged, making a mistake or others noticing their anxious behaviour. This, in turn, can create a fear of behaving in an embarrassing or humiliating way, which leads to withdrawal from social situations.

One of the worst cases we encountered was a lady who ran out of a hair salon with her hair dripping wet as the social interaction with the hairdresser was just too much to bear. We met another woman whose social anxiety meant she couldn't walk through the door of her doctor's surgery, despite her serious health condition.

CASE STUDY
Karen: Extreme Social Anxiety

Karen had severe social anxiety, which she described as a phobia of 'dealing with people'.

Karen worked with her husband David as a school cleaner – the only job she could find where she felt safe that there would be no one else around. If she ever walked into a classroom and saw a teacher who had stayed late at school, she would literally break down and cry. Karen was struggling to hold on to her job, and because of her fear of social interaction she relied on David for everything.

They rarely left the house, and she felt a huge amount of guilt for not seeing her children and grandchildren, despite them only living minutes away – the last photograph she had with any of them was taken ten years before.

For years Karen had tried medication, counselling and self-help books, but nothing had worked. She was desperate to get over her social anxiety, but she felt powerless to control her fears.

When Karen came to our clinic for therapy, we asked her why people scared her. She said she feared she would say or do something stupid, and that they would judge her.

Prior to our therapy, we had asked Karen's family to send us letters for her. We read them to Karen during the session. One of her grandchildren wrote: *'I love you, Nan, but we don't get to see you much. I want to have dinner with you and to go* and feed the ducks.' Karen was upset to hear this because she hadn't realised her grandchildren actually wanted to see her. Karen's son wrote: 'Mum, I think you are very special. Since the children were born, we haven't seen you as much as we would like to, and the kids need you in their lives. We all miss the way you were; a happy, loving mother.' Karen's daughter wrote: 'Mum, you will probably find our letters hard to read, but we need you to know how much love and support we have for you. It is really hard knowing that you have missed out on so much in all our lives. We want nothing more than for you to enjoy having time with the grandchildren. I personally would love to have a girly day out for lunch and go shopping, but I know at the moment that is too much. Please know we are all here for you, but most of all we just want our mum back.'

Karen was shocked as she hadn't felt she was important to her family. She agreed there was no judgement from them. For years she had believed something that was untrue, and now she was hearing – and having to face – facts. Prior to our meeting, her family had been treading on eggshells, not knowing the best way to deal with Karen, and therefore they had not been as candid about their feelings with her.

We made a list with Karen of all the people who mattered in her life. We asked how many of them were judging her, taking into consideration that she hadn't found any time for any of them over the last decade. She looked through the list and revealed that none of them were judging her, despite her having missed so many milestones in their lives.

We told Karen that she faced a choice: to believe something that wasn't true and continue to walk away from her family, or to look at the facts and take her family back! Her family loved her so much that they were prepared to hurt themselves, and keep their distance, to make her life more bearable. Karen had never considered this before, and her perspective of how loved she was began to change.

We asked Karen who had taken away her self-esteem.

Karen revealed that she had been bullied at school. At one point the whole class had turned against her and stopped talking to her for two weeks.

We asked Karen to look at this painful situation again but to consider an alternative – and likely more factual – positive perspective. Karen recalled that she hadn't been entirely ignored, and it hadn't actually been everyone in the class who had refused to speak to her. When the bullying stopped, Karen had continued to be unkind to herself.

Karen was finally able to accept that she was a very loved lady. Later that same day, she was able to meet her whole family in a restaurant, which would have been unthinkable before. For the first time in a decade, they were all together.

Karen now sees her family weekly. She loves spending time with her grandchildren and is a manager in a department store, dealing face to face with staff and the public every day.

Glossophobia (Fear of Public Speaking)

Glossophobia – the medical term for a fear of public speaking – is thought to be the number-one fear in the world. It is considered a social phobia or social anxiety disorder, and a recent YouGov survey suggested that 20 per cent of Britons are too afraid to speak publicly.[17] The survey also revealed that women are twice as likely as men to be 'very afraid' of public speaking.

Glossophobia can also be described as stage fright or performance anxiety and it holds people back in many different ways. It can ruin events that should be positive and exciting experiences, such as birthday parties, a best man's speech or walking down the aisle as a bride.

Surprisingly, research shows that people with severe social anxiety say they would rather die than speak in front of a group of people.[18]

CASE STUDY
Maria: Severe Glossophobia

Meeting bubbly, confident company director Maria, it was hard to believe that she had a problem with public speaking. Maria explained that she had no issue talking to one, two, three or even four people – but any more than that and she would panic and faint, so she had to employ someone to speak on her behalf at business meetings. She felt that her fear was holding her back and that she was letting herself and her team down. Maria had the knowledge and skills to expand her business, but in order to do so she would need to present and pitch in meetings to secure bigger clients.

We asked Maria to tell us how she felt if she had to make a speech. She said she was worried she would 'mess it up and embarrass [myself]'. She had used the same words earlier, and for us, they were a key piece of evidence in determining how her fear started.

We asked when in her life she had 'messed up and embarrassed herself'. She immediately responded: 'When I fainted as I was about to deliver a presentation for a business contract.' We explained to Maria that, for her to have had this phobic response at that moment, the phobia must already have been present.

We asked Maria to think back to when she was a little girl. Had she ever spoken in front of a group, become 'embarrassed' and 'messed up'? It was evident from Maria's eye movements that she was searching through a magnitude of schemas, when suddenly it came flooding back: 'The Brownies!'

The Brownies are the section of the long-running Girlguiding UK organisation for girls aged seven to ten. To officially become a Brownie, Maria would have had to stand up in front of her group to recite the 'Brownie Promise'.

Maria's mum had been given a sheet of paper with Maria's lines, which Maria had learned by heart with pride. With the girls all sitting in a circle, this was Maria's big moment. Excitedly, she stood up and recited the words impeccably. She still remembered them word for word more than forty years later. Back then, little Maria, beaming with pride, was delighted with her efforts. The group leader (known as Brown Owl) nodded approvingly and said, 'Well done, Maria, that was wonderful. Now can you read the second part?'

What second part? Maria had not been told about a second part!

Needless to say, this moment of joy instantly changed into a moment of complete and utter trauma. Maria was now standing in front of the group, getting more and more embarrassed as she had no words at all for Brown Owl. In that moment, Maria's glossophobia was created. This experience and all the bad feelings associated with it had now become the foundation reference for any future occasion where she had to speak to more than four people. Prior to our meeting, Maria had no idea that this event had been the culprit. In fact, Maria hadn't thought about the Brownies for years. She was very distressed to recall the embarrassment and shame she had felt at that time. It was obvious that she was still seeing the event through the eyes of her seven-year-old self, feeling the same horror she had felt standing in front of Brown Owl and the room full of Brownies. This explained why the seven-year-old Maria had activated an airtight, high-alert protective instruction to save her from ever having to go through that pain, shame and embarrassment ever again.

To help Maria, we had to change her perspective of that event, helping her to see it for what it actually was and not how it felt at the time so as to condition and reconstruct her negative schema.

We revisited the event. Maria confirmed that her mum had not been given the 'second part', and therefore Maria had only learned what she had been given. We asked Maria if she had complied with everything she had been asked to do. Maria said yes.

We then asked if she had been excited to recite 'the Promise'. She said she had put so much work into learning it, because she wanted Brown Owl to see how committed she was to the Brownies.

We asked Maria if she had not only complied, but also excelled at delivering her lines. She said yes. We asked if she could have learned the second part and recited it just as well as the first, if it had been given to her. She said yes, of course. So, we asked, who was actually at fault for the entire situation? 'Brown Owl,' Maria said. Who actually messed up that day by forgetting to give the second part of the recital to her mum, and therefore who should have been embarrassed? Maria responded, 'Brown Owl.'

With this epiphany, Maria said, 'I had never thought of it like that before. I did what I was supposed to, and not only that, I did a great job.'

The following day, we sat in a lecture theatre at the University of East Anglia, watching Maria deliver a humorous, engaging and informative twenty-minute talk to 350 business students. Maria had every person in the theatre mesmerised. In fact, she was so confident and engaging that the professor of business studies asked if she would come back and speak to another group. We were absolutely overjoyed!

'All the great speakers were bad speakers at first.'
Ralph Waldo Emerson

The Origin of Social Anxiety and Glossophobia

The good news is that glossophobia and social anxiety are not genetic or biological conditions. As you have seen in Maria's story, they are learned behaviours, most often acquired in childhood, particularly between the ages of five and thirteen. So a fear of public speaking does not have to be a lifelong affliction.

Whether you are socially anxious, find big groups overwhelming in general or cannot speak publicly to more than a few people, the likely culprits are:

* **Being bullied by someone at school, home or work, and as a result wanting to disappear from view or keep a low profile.**

* **Being laughed at and humiliated because of something you said or mispronounced – for example, when reading out loud in class, such as an English lesson.**

* **Forgetting lines in a school play or assembly.**

* **Being made to feel worthless and inadequate by an abusive parent, friend or partner.**

* **Low self-esteem leading you to compare yourself to others and chastise yourself for not being as good, clever, articulate or beautiful as them.**

* **Comparing your life negatively to other people's lives – for example, on social media – overlooking the fact that these images are usually enhanced or exaggerated, and that people rarely post details of the bad things in their lives.**

* **Comparing your possessions to others' and feeling like a failure if they appear to have more than you materially.**

* Experiencing immense embarrassment.

* Copied behaviour from a parent or close family member.

* Being chastised or shouted at. For example, in class at school or in front of friends by a parent.

* Being told by a teacher that you will not amount to anything.

* Seeing someone else laughed at or humiliated when speaking in public, and not wanting that to happen to you.

* Lack of preparation or having had a bad experience due to lack of preparation.

* Being silenced by a parent (the 'children should be seen and not heard' rule) or being in the shadow of a more confident, headstrong sibling.

To overcome your social anxiety or fear of public speaking, you need to:

1 Locate the origin of your belief. Was it learned? Copied? Was it as a result of an unpleasant event?

2 Consider your perception of the originating event/events that contributed to your social anxiety or fear of public speaking.

3 Challenge the origin of your belief to alter your perception of the memory positively.

4 Practise and rehearse being confident.

5 Build genuine self-confidence with practice and by following the exercises we suggest, including our Sighing Technique later in this chapter (see page 178).

> *Few people are entirely comfortable with public speaking, but with practice and rehearsal everyone can be.*

Challenging the Origin

> 'There are only two types of speakers in the world: the nervous and liars.'
>
> **Mark Twain**

If you suffer from social anxiety or glossophobia, the first step to permanently changing this learned behaviour is to consider who first made you feel this way. What happened? Who belittled you, laughed at you or made you feel inferior or foolish? This is the root of your issue; it's why you feel the need to keep away from people or feel unable to share your voice and knowledge. Your reaction is quite simply you protecting yourself from these past negative memories and preventing those emotions from happening again. However, please realise that it is unfair to penalise yourself and deprive others of your company or knowledge because of the actions of one or a few events in your past. You are expecting everyone to be no different to the perpetrator(s) of your issue and, as we established earlier, this is both unfair and inaccurate.

Consider the originating event or events that led to your fear of humiliation in social settings. What you believed then is unlikely to be true now, or was possibly never true at all, just a misinterpretation. Could you have misunderstood the situation? Was what happened even about you? Was your perception of your shame exaggerated due to being a child? Was it actually someone or some people who made you feel bad and were you truthfully not to blame?

From our experience in treating social anxiety, we know that the likelihood is that your issue began in childhood. Ask yourself, as an adult, when would you ever take advice on a serious and important issue from a child? Can you see that, if your behaviour continues to be dictated by your child self, this is what is happening?

Also, be fair to the adults in your life now. Your current expectation is that if you mess up, they will respond like children, too (just like when this issue was created). You imagine that a room full of adults would laugh, shout out, tease you or cause a scene just like at school, when children are trying to get respite or distraction from a boring lesson. Would adults you meet in your daily life ever do this? We suggest it is pretty unlikely!

If you are suffering with glossophobia, why did you choose to blame public speaking rather than the true cause of your trauma? If your fear stems from a teacher who humiliated you in class, then it wasn't speaking out that caused your discomfort, it was the teacher being unprofessional. To change your perception and condition your schema, you need to re-examine the original event, seeing it for what it was and not how it felt in that moment. If the teacher reprimanded you and you were embarrassed, then perhaps the teacher was just having a bad day, or in a class of thirty pupils mistakenly thought you were responsible for something.

If you misread something when reading a book out in class, and the class laughed, ask yourself, realistically, what are the chances of you having to speak publicly in front of those very same people ever again? It's unfair to judge adults today for the behaviour of your classmates. This very situation happened to Nik at school and put him off public speaking for a long time. And yet now he confidently speaks in front of many hundreds of people and, when on television, millions. Take heart that you can overcome this issue yourself.

Finally, we'd like to ask if you remember someone messing up at school. When someone else misread something in class and everyone laughed, would it be fair to say you all laughed, even you? But it is likely that no one meant any malice, and you and the other children probably cannot even remember the incident or persons involved. This is likely the same for your own traumatising incident. People are too consumed with themselves, their own lives and issues to relive yours. They let your incident go there and then, and now you can, too.

CASE STUDY
Annie: Speaking Out

As we approached the confidence element of our workshop, we asked for a volunteer who would feel very uncomfortable coming up on stage with us but would be willing to come and join us for the purpose of demonstrating our technique to address this.

As the odd hand wavered, Annie caught our eye. Her hand went up partially, then promptly went back down, and then up again, and then down again. She wanted help, but the fear schema in her unconscious mind was overpowering her conscious decision to come forward, causing an internal conflict. We asked Annie if she'd like to join us on stage.

As she took a seat on the stage, we asked how she was feeling. Annie replied, 'I'm very nervous,' and as she wiped her hands on her skirt she added, 'and I'm sweaty and clammy and my heart is racing.' We asked her to score her anxiety on a level of zero to ten. Before we could explain further, Annie snapped back, 'Ten, definitely ten.'

Annie said, 'I feel such a fool and you are going to think I'm a fraud, but I am a school teacher. I can speak to my students, but not to adults, and being sat here, I'm petrified.'

Annie went on to say that she loved her job; she knew she was a good teacher and had no problem at all speaking to her class, but found speaking in front of adults – such as during school assembly – impossible.

When asking Annie about the origins of her issue, she could not recall a specific incident. However, when we asked her about her parents and childhood, Annie told us that her father had been in the military and his motto was that children should be seen and not heard. When they had adult visitors, both Annie and her sister were told to sit quietly and only speak when they were spoken to. It appeared that from this childhood experience, Annie had created a schema that she could speak to children, but not adults.

When we asked Annie how this revelation felt, she began to laugh and said, 'That totally makes sense.' She further explained how nervous she would become at parents' evenings for her students.

We asked Annie whether she went to the playground or the staff room during the school break periods. Annie replied, 'The staff room.' We asked why she did this, rather than go in the playground with the children. Annie thought for a little while and, with some confusion, responded, 'Because I am staff?' We challenged Annie's response and said, 'But surely with your view on your situation, you should go and play out with the kids, as you are not able to speak to adults.' Annie had an instant lightbulb moment and said, 'Oh damn, I'm all grown up, aren't I?' Everyone, including Annie, laughed.

It was evident that Annie had had a significant shift in her perspective, which was visible in her body language.

We asked her to once again look out at the audience and tell us how she felt. Annie gave a beaming smile and joked, 'I can stay on the stage if you like, I feel absolutely fine.'

How to Make a Positive Difference

I've tried so many kinds of help/interventions and meds. Now I'm med-free, work full time in a highly stressful job, and am happy and confident. The Speakmans helped more than anything else.

Emma

Addressing the origin of a behaviour is always the quickest and most effective way to change it for good. Our thoughts create our feelings, so altering your thoughts will alter your feelings.

It is likely that as a child you may have looked at certain foods and thought, 'That looks disgusting.' Perhaps olives, oysters, Stilton cheese, an artichoke or Waldorf salad? Just from the food's appearance, you create a schema. Then, as you get older, someone persuades you to try it or you inadvertently eat an olive in another dish and enjoy it. Suddenly, based on this new positive evidence, you have better thoughts about this food and your schema is positively conditioned. You will not need to work on liking that food in the future, or do exercises to make the food more enjoyable or remind yourself that you like it now.

Positively challenging your originating negative schema will have the same effect. However, here are some further tips to help you with social anxiety or speaking out, whether publicly or just to one person. Like a muscle, the more you exercise your confidence in public speaking, the stronger you will feel. Here are some confidence exercises to give you strength in speaking out.

Rehearsal and belief

To help overcome your fear, consider rehearsing before you socialise, speak out or speak publicly. Close your eyes and strongly visualise yourself delivering a perfect speech and receiving a warm reception from your audience or interacting with an engaged group of friends. This helps you to gain confidence in advance, and will build your belief in your abilities.

Doing this a number of times gives your brain the message that you have already overcome your fear and done the task, and that it went really well. Your brain cannot tell the difference between something you have actually experienced and something you have strongly visualised or rehearsed.

Belief is powerful, and therefore we need you to rehearse to believe in yourself.

Some years ago, on a TV show we worked on, on Channel M, we met Dr David Hamilton and he told us about a pain control study and the effects of placebos. Ten people who were in severe pain and were given morphine to control it were asked if they would like to participate in a study for a groundbreaking new type of morphine, which they could try out.

They all agreed. Every day a doctor visited them at home and injected them with this new wonder morphine for three days. However, it was actually just a slightly higher dose of normal morphine. All reported being pain free.

On day four the participants were injected with a placebo that was simply a coloured saline solution that looked like morphine. That continued for an entire month. By the end of the month, nine out of the ten remained pain free, the tenth stating they felt considerably better but did have a small element of pain. This experiment is a testament to the absolute power of belief. Because the participants believed they were being injected with a new painkilling wonder drug, the majority remained pain free.

'An ounce of practice is worth more than tons of preaching.'

Gandhi

Sighing Technique

When your brain is producing these [alpha] waves, it's responding to activities like meditation and rest that can reduce your stress levels and help you feel calmer.

Healthline.com[19]

Over the many years we have been working in therapy, we noticed a consistent similarity at the point of change, when our client had their eureka moment and were cured of their issue. This similarity was an unconscious, emotive sigh.

With that in mind, we wondered whether a forced sigh may have a positive effect, and so some years ago we created our Sighing Technique, which we went on to experiment with, both in our clinic and at our workshops, with incredibly positive results.

Although not necessarily offering the participant an immediate 'cure', it did offer an immediate calm. And our daughter Liv, while studying for her degree in Experimental Psychology and Neuroscience at the University of Oxford, pointed out that there's a significant link between sighing and the creation of alpha waves in the brain.

Alpha waves are created during restful relaxation, offering a feeling of calm. Studies have shown an increased creation of alpha waves during meditation and mindfulness, but although helpful, due to the time, space and set-up required, neither are a practical solution if you are having anxiety or panic attacks in public places, or feeling anxious moments before delivering a speech or presentation at work.

Our Sighing Technique is a simple but effective coping technique. It acts as a physiological and psychological reset, signalling to your brain and body that the task has been completed.

Use this technique again for a quick and effective boost of confidence moments before having to go out, speak out, socialise or speak in public. We sometimes use this technique ourselves seconds before we are hosting a live show or appearing on television. We would therefore like to share our Sighing Technique with you now.

> **Alpha brainwaves are dominant during quietly flowing thoughts, and in some meditative states. Alpha is the resting state for the brain.**
>
> **Brainworks Neurotherapy**[20]

The Sighing Technique is simple, and can be done anywhere, sitting or standing.

1 Think about whatever it is you are about to do, or your feeling of anxiety and discomfort, and score this out of ten so you know that the negative feeling is reducing.

2 Put your hands together in front of you, interlocking your fingers so they are clasped together (this is not essential but it's better if you can).

3 Now do a large, exaggerated and emotive sigh – this is sigh one.

4 Wait a few seconds, then repeat the sigh and let your shoulders drop down – this is sigh two.

5 Wait a few seconds, then repeat the sigh, allowing yourself to sink into your seat, or relax your body if standing – this is sigh three.

6   Wait a few seconds, then repeat the sigh, this time dropping your clasped hands down to your thighs – this is sigh four.

7   Score how you feel. You should now feel calm or significantly calmer. If not, repeat sighs three and four, closing your eyes if you prefer to do so.

We often sigh when something 'difficult' is over, so thinking about whatever is troubling you and sighing is likely to give you that same sense of achievement and relief you'd get from completing a task, therefore offering another positive benefit of our technique. Ensure that your sighs are emotive sighs. Sigh out loud (if possible) and engage your whole body.

Sigh to reduce the negative emotionality of a schema

You can also use our Sighing Technique to address negative memories and events on your questionnaire and timeline.

Picture the event and score your fear or anxiety out of ten. Then, while holding that picture in your mind's eye, carry out the Sighing Technique.

Over-sighing can make you feel lightheaded, so only carry this out in increments of six or seven sighs, while monitoring the score of the negative emotion associated to that memory or event and taking breaks in between.

Keep using the Sighing Technique until thinking about the event gives you no fear or a significantly reduced level of fear.

Prepare

> 'It usually takes me more than three weeks to prepare for a good impromptu speech.'
>
> **Mark Twain**

Write down some topics you can talk about confidently and use them to start conversations when you're socialising, such as popular TV shows, things that are happening in the world or hobbies you're passionate about. Having a few topics at hand can act like a security blanket. Once you build a rapport with someone, it's amazing how quickly your insecurities and anxieties can disappear. One of the most common rapport builders in the UK is talking about the weather!

If giving a speech, research your content so you have confidence in your knowledge, then practise the delivery as often as possible so that you become aware of any potential stumbling blocks.

Gaining rapport

From constantly analysing human behaviour, and paying attention to interactions in our own social and professional circles, we can tell you that the secret to rapport is commonality. The moment you can latch on to something the other person likes or is interested in, which also interests you, a door opens to an easy, relaxed conversation.

Here are some examples of conversations to help you build rapport and start a conversation:

Attending a wedding or party
Are you here for the bride or groom?
Where do you know .... from?
How long have you known ....?
I met .... and have known them for .... years.
I remember when I first met .... they ....

A stranger in a bar or restaurant
(As music is usually playing, try ....) Who is this?
Do you like this song? What kind of music are you into?
What's your favourite drink?

Is this your local? Where else would you recommend?
Why?

On a date
What kind of music do you like?
What's your favourite food?
Can you cook? Do you have a signature dish? How do you
make it?
What's your favourite movie?
If you could go anywhere in the world, where would that
be and why?
If you had a time machine, what era would you go back to
and why?

Meeting new work colleagues/first day at work
How long have you worked here?
Is there anything I need to know?
Where's the best place to grab lunch nearby?

Mirror and match

You can also gain immediate rapport and start on a better
footing with someone new by mirroring and matching the
person you are engaging with. This means paying attention
to the person's posture, body language and terminology. You
are aiming to subtly mirror and match them to build rapport.

For instance, people find it effective to repeat some of the
words that the other has used:

Person A 'I find that parties can be stressful situations.'
Person B 'Parties can be stressful.'
Person A 'Yes! Do you think so, too?'

This is a particularly effective technique for interviews
and work situations, as it demonstrates that you are really
listening and not just waiting for your turn to speak.

You must start with small and subtle adjustments so as not to make it glaringly obvious what you are doing, but if you do have social anxiety, this will not only help distract you positively, but also help you gain rapport.

Use props

Props can help to offer a distraction, assurance or temporary relief from social anxiety.

Give yourself as many comfort props as you need in situations you know are stressful for you. When you feel you are going out into a worrying situation alone and unarmed, this can make you feel vulnerable. For example, if you're delivering a speech, try using index cards to read from. This is perfectly acceptable and an effective prompt. It also helps if there is somebody in your social circle who you love and trust in the audience, so that you can direct your eyes to them for reassurance and comfort during a talk or speech.

Having some photographs on your telephone is also a good prop. This may be a picture of your pet doing something funny, a place you visited and loved, a picture that made you laugh from social media or your favourite car. Not only can holding your phone relieve fidgety hands during a conversation that may give away your anxiety, but you now have a prop for a conversation point or an ice breaker.

Finally, our Pressure-point Technique is something you can take with you anywhere – no one will ever see it and it will provide a boost of confidence, too.

Pressure-point Technique

An acupressure point exists in your hand known as the Union Valley point, which is believed to help reduce anxiety and stress, and has proved very effective for people we have helped. This technique offers a great prop and comfort for social situations or when delivering a speech to a group of people. Don't forget, the more times you socialise and speak well in public, the more evidence you collect that you can do it, and therefore your confidence will build and the use of props will no longer be necessary.

Here's what to do:

* **Sit comfortably.**

* **Find the stress-relieving pressure point in your hand (use whichever hand feels comfortable). The point is just below the webbing between your thumb and index finger.**

* **Using the thumb of your other hand, apply gentle pressure.**

* **Take slow, deep breaths through your nose and out of your mouth (you can close your eyes if you prefer).**

* **Apply gentle, firm pressure in a circular motion, thinking about things you have done with confidence and imagining yourself doing your imminent speech or social event confidently (repeat these thoughts, breathing slowly and deeply, with your eyes closed if you can).**

* **Do this for five or ten minutes, repeating daily.**

You have now set up a confidence trigger within your pressure point on your hand. This point can now be used as your prop and support whenever out socially, interacting or speaking publicly. It is very subtle and will merely look like you're holding your hands together. Don't forget to keep the point topped up, repeating this quick technique and adding new memories, confident events and tasks you have completed until you no longer need a prop.

Please believe us when we say that fear of speaking publicly is one of the most common fears we encounter in our practice, and also one of the most easily fixed. We hope you will soon feel much more confident in speaking out.

Truly inspirational and life-changing day.
   It was emotional but amazing. Thank you for helping me to grab my life with both hands.
   You're an exceptional couple.

Amanda

8

Shyness and Blushing

Eva and Nik, you have changed my life. I'm so grateful for what you have both done for me. Shortly after speaking to you I noticed how completely different I felt. I'll never forget what you have done for me. I'm living my life now, without a fear of blushing. Thank you both so much for everything.

My eternal gratitude.

Liza

There is often confusion about the difference between shyness and social anxiety, but the truth is that these are quite different things. Social anxiety is an acquired behaviour that can be traced back to a triggering event, while shyness is a personality trait. Many shy people do not feel the negative emotions and feelings that accompany social anxiety disorder – they live a perfectly normal life and do not necessarily view their shyness as a negative trait. While it is true that many of those with social anxiety are also shy, it is worth stating that shyness is not a prerequisite for social anxiety.

In our practice, we have come across shy people who would nonetheless consider speaking publicly and would happily speak to people if spoken to. While other shy people would feel anxious to speak publicly or go out and speak to people.

Whether socially anxious or shy, most people are self-diagnosed in both cases, and therefore the label used is generally based on the opinion and choice of words used by the individual as opposed to an accurate diagnosis.

Having devoted a full chapter to social anxiety, we anticipate that a combination of the advice in Chapter 7 and the advice in this chapter will help you. For the purposes of offering additional solutions to help with shyness, we have differentiated the topics as follows:

Social Anxiety

Our definition of a person who is socially anxious is someone who experiences feelings of anxiety and fear at the prospect of speaking out or socialising. Socially anxious people would prefer to avoid such situations.

We would expect someone with social anxiety to most often have a definitive uncomfortable or traumatic experience that led to the creation of their social anxiety.

Treatment for social anxiety:

* **Address the cause by positively restructuring your perception of the originating event.**

* **Build confidence with practice.**

* **Use techniques and approaches as suggested in Chapter 7.**

Shyness

Our definition of shyness, for the purpose of this chapter, is someone who may be uncomfortable or nervous when speaking out or socialising, but who, once familiar with the person and circumstances, gains confidence and feels comfortable. Shy people will not avoid social situations, but usually prefer to allow others to talk rather than initiate conversations themselves. A shy person may prefer to be a listener or observer, but will be a willing and able participant if spoken to.

People who are shy are often quiet due to conditioning from their upbringing and home environment as opposed to a traumatic event. As we have said, many shy people are perfectly happy being shy. But for those who would like to feel more confident, there are some simple tools available.

Treatment for shyness:

* **Techniques to create new behaviours.**

* **Practise to make the techniques habits.**

* **Rehearse topics for conversation.**

CASE STUDY
Martin: Shyness

We met a lovely family at our workshop that comprised of a mum, her older daughter and younger son, Martin.

As we chatted, it was evident that the mum and daughter were confident and sociable. However, Martin was not forthcoming with conversation at all. His body language was very closed, with rounded shoulders and eyes mostly directed at the floor. Martin spoke when spoken to, but did not participate in conversations with the same enthusiasm as his mum and sister.

After the mum and sister had finished telling us about their day and reason for attending, we asked Martin why he had come along. Instantly, the mum and sister replied on his behalf, telling us that Martin was quite shy and came to gain more confidence and motivation. We looked at Martin and asked, 'Have you enjoyed your day so far?' Martin responded that he had. We asked whether there was something specific that he enjoyed, to which his sister responded, 'We've loved everything, and the Mirror Technique was amazing.'

The conversation went on, with our questions most often answered by Martin's mum and sister. Knowing that the family standing in front of us had come to our workshop to improve their lives in some way, we had to be honest about the dynamic we saw, even though we felt that the mum may initially be upset over what she was about to hear.

We started by commending the mum on her lovely children, but then went on to add that it was evident why Martin was 'shy'. They all looked with eager anticipation for an answer to their quandary. Looking at the mum and sister, we said, 'Look, guys, we understand that you are acting out of kindness, but your kindness is totally killing Martin's confidence.' We explained to them that what they had done, and were still doing, was taking Martin's voice away and reducing his need to interact with others.

After our short discussion, we highlighted:

* **That the sister, as the elder sibling, had the ability to speak before Martin, therefore she had taken the role of spokesperson for both of them. This was natural and not done with any negative intent.**

* **That the sister speaking for Martin had resulted in Martin not learning to interact as confidently. To this day, his sister (and also his mum) were responding for him.**

* **That Martin had created a habit of allowing his mum and sister to speak for him.**

* **That Martin as an adult was being polite so as not to speak over his mum and sister.**

* That the mum was being kind, answering on his behalf to protect her son from any discomfort.

* That it was possible that Martin was not shy, just polite and inexperienced in social interactions.

Martin's sister looked shocked, and immediately said, 'Oh no, I feel so bad.' We explained that no one should feel guilty in this situation, as everyone's intentions were caring and loving.

> *You should only feel guilty if your actions are done with malice or intent to hurt.*

A conversation ensued, and Martin confirmed that he was neither upset nor angry with his mum or sister. In fact, he felt liberated to know that 'I am not shy, just polite and inexperienced' – an affirmation that he said he would now use. We further shared some techniques to use while building new habits.

Techniques to Improve Shyness

Consider the cause

If you feel your shyness is problematic, and if it causes you to lack confidence, consider the origin of this feeling. Shyness may be a personality trait, but it can also be exacerbated by your life experience. Did someone always speak for you, as Martin's sister did? Did you copy a shy parent and minimise your social interactions? Once you have discovered the origin of your problematic shyness, you can begin to challenge it by reminding yourself that you are not necessarily shy, but just lacking in experience of social interaction. And that is easy to fix.

Practice

Confidence will build from practice. Any new skill you learn, whether riding a bike, driving a car or even making a meal, comes with practice, and being more forthcoming in conversations is no different. To learn new habits, you have to make a conscious decision to practise new behaviours. A great place to start is to make conversation with every person you interact with. This includes shop assistants, bartenders, people at work, at the gym, on the bus or at the train station. An easy start is to compliment something they have or are wearing, or your surroundings. Once you start a conversation, it just flows from there. You can make a game of it – perhaps set yourself a goal to see how many conversations you can have with strangers in the space of one day.

Affirmation

Knowing the origin of your behaviour, use daily affirmations such as, 'I am not shy, I am polite and inexperienced.'

Fake it

Pretending to be confident will help you adopt your new confident behaviours. Imagine if you had to force yourself to use a different accent. After a period of time, you would start to adopt elements of that accent even when you stopped trying. The same is true for confidence. A great way to fake it is to adopt a character – for example, think of an actor or television character who appears confident to you, and

pretend to be them in situations when you feel nervous.
A shy actor that we met in our clinic used this technique.
He was confident at work when playing a character, but
struggled with being himself in interviews and at red carpet
events. So he literally imagined stepping into an image of
Will Smith – taking on what he believed to be Will Smith's
character, physiology and body language, using him as a
security blanket to become more confident.

Body language

People who are shy usually have closed-off body language.
They look down at the ground, hunch their shoulders and
do everything they can to appear smaller and even invisible.
To counter this, practise open body language. Hold your
shoulders back, make eye contact with everyone and hold
your head up high. Project your voice clearly and create the
habit of shaking hands, hugging, fist bumping or giving a
high-five to friends and family.

Blushing

*I would like to say a huge thank you for your help with
my blushing. I cannot thank you enough. You are the
most personable, friendly and uplifting people I have ever
met and I know you are going to help me change my life
forever.*

Lindsay

Blushing, for many, is one of the most traumatic
consequences of lacking confidence and the most significant
worst-case scenario, because it cannot be hidden from
others. Blushing is shyness and social anxiety made visible,
and that can be very difficult for those who suffer from it,

not least because being aware that you are blushing makes you blush even more.

We have worked with numerous people who have created a phobia of blushing, and others who have even gone as far as considering surgery or having Botox injections as a solution.

Blushing, however, is a symptom, rather than an issue in itself. We all blush from time to time, but when we address a debilitating fear of blushing, our therapeutic approach is always the same, and that is to address the cause so as to negate the symptom.

Physiologically, blushing is a response to an emotional trigger, which activates your fight-or-flight response. The adrenaline released by your body causes the capillaries that carry blood to your skin to widen, and this is the reason you appear flushed. The resolution, therefore, is to appease the fight-or-flight response, and offer enough countering positive evidence to allow your protection response to step down.

CASE STUDY
Molly: Blushing

Molly asked for our help with her phobia of blushing, known as erythrophobia. She told us that she had never been the most outspoken of people, but she was perfectly happy until, after a very embarrassing incident, she had developed a phobia of blushing. This fear was causing her to isolate herself from her friends and the world in general.

Molly was only twenty-six when we met her, and as we spoke about her issue we explained that blushing is a natural reaction, often as a consequence of an event that activates our internal protection response. We also explained that natural blushing can be more noticeable depending on both the number of blood capillaries and their closeness to the surface of the skin.

Molly was quick to say that she knew the exact moment when her issue began, and she shared an incident from when she was nineteen years of age. Molly had started university and told a fellow student, Rebecca, in confidence that she was attracted to Oliver, one of the young men in their group. Molly had not really dated before, and was a little shy and inexperienced in talking to boys.

On a particularly hot summer's day, Molly was in the park with a group of seven or eight other students, which included both Rebecca (the girl Molly had confided in) and Oliver (the boy she liked). As they chatted and sunbathed on the grass, the conversation moved to dating and whether anyone had caught anyone's eye since starting university. Molly was absolutely mortified when Rebecca mocked, 'I know who Molly has her eye on,' and then directed her stare at Oliver for all to see. Molly was devastated. Not only had her friend broken her trust, but she had also humiliated Molly and embarrassed both her and Oliver.

As everyone started to giggle and tease her, someone in the group made the statement, 'Awww, look, it must be true, Molly's blushing.' Knowing that if this were true she couldn't hide it, Molly felt backed into a corner and wished she could disappear.

From that moment on Molly noticed she was avoiding situations in which she might be embarrassed. She was avoiding blushing at all costs. As the months and years passed, her fear of blushing had accelerated, and now, seven years later, she labelled herself as someone suffering with erythrophobia (a phobia of blushing).

We explained to Molly that the cause was the behavioural schema she had created at university in the park. Molly agreed and said, 'I know that, but how do I stop it?'

We asked Molly a number of questions, which included whether she had been able to go to that park again after that event? Had she been able to speak to Rebecca? Had she been able to associate with the group? Had she spoken to Oliver? Molly confirmed that she had, although it was never the same again with Rebecca.

We explained to Molly that she was fearing and blaming the wrong thing. Molly was confused, so we added, 'You're avoiding blushing as though that is what made you feel bad that day, but who actually made you feel bad?' Molly responded, 'Oh yes, that is true, it was Rebecca.'

We asked, 'Who caused you to blush?'

Molly confirmed that it had been Rebecca.

We asked why she didn't have a phobia of Rebecca, as that was who she should have worried about. Molly laughed.

We then asked Molly if anyone before or since had pointed out that she was blushing. Molly said that they had not.

We asked Molly whether she was sure she had even blushed that day. Had she seen it in a mirror? Molly confirmed that she had not.

We mentioned that in our experience, playground teasing would often include the words, 'Oh, you must like him/her because you're blushing,' even if the person was not blushing at all. Molly confirmed that she had heard that statement, and agreed it was something children might say even if the person were not blushing. We asked, 'Could this just have been a little immature teasing? Have you considered that you didn't even blush?'

Molly thought for a moment and said, 'I guess I may not have blushed at all. It was obvious she was trying to have fun at my expense or perhaps push me and Oliver together.'

We then said, 'And even if you had blushed, did it stop that group of friends wanting to be your friend? Did they turn away from you? Did Oliver stop talking to you? Did it put everyone off you?' Molly confirmed that it hadn't; in fact, they were all still in touch, and she had even dated Oliver for a while.

We asked again, 'So even if you did blush, did everyone go off you?'

Molly firmly said, 'No.'

Finally, we asked Molly to repeat again where she had been that day, how long they had been there and what they had been doing. Molly confirmed, 'We were sunbathing in the park all afternoon.' We asked, 'Molly, might you have had a bit of sunburn?' Molly burst out laughing, to the point of tears, and said, 'OMG, I looked like a blooming beetroot! We'd all been out all day with no sun cream! We were students and it was our first time from home.'

We asked, 'Molly, why are you laughing?' She replied, 'I was probably sunburnt that day, so even if I had been blushing, no one would've been able to tell as I was so red anyway.' This huge realisation, coupled with her laughter, had completely changed Molly's view of events, herself and her fear of blushing.

Six months afterwards, Molly got in touch to say that she felt a weight had lifted off her shoulders immediately and that her life had changed for the better since she overcame her phobia. She realised that her anticipation of blushing had been her biggest issue, but now the thought of blushing made her smile, because if she was red it was most likely sunburn. She also realised that she had blamed blushing for her discomfort, when she should have blamed Rebecca.

Addressing blushing

Blushing can literally light up your face and illuminate your beauty.

It is important to acknowledge and discount other causes of looking flushed and rosy-cheeked – for example, hormonal imbalance, rosacea or other skin conditions, overheating or feeling unwell. If you think there may be a medical condition behind your issues with blushing, please make an appointment with a doctor or specialist. However, if your blushing is as a consequence of an emotional trigger, it will help to address the trigger that caused you to blush initially, while using positive evidence to challenge your negative association with blushing.

Look through your timeline for the earliest occasion when you recall blushing. This may be the foundation on which your issue has been built. Subsequent events on your timeline when you blushed are probably all a consequence of that first event; they sit on top of that foundation, reinforcing and strengthening your fear-of-blushing schema. This means that, if you address the instillation of the fear, you remove the foundation, so all the later events fall apart, too. Your aim is to re-examine the originating event and look for alternative, more positive interpretations, just as we did with Molly.

When looking at the event, consider:

* **Who caused you to blush?**

* **Were you actually blushing or was someone just teasing you?**

* **Was the blushing to blame for how you felt?**

* **Was it blushing that was the problem or was it the person or event that caused you to activate your fight-or-flight response?**

* **What was the person's true motive? Were they trying to deflect attention from themselves? Did they have a secret crush on you?**

You should then look for positive information, such as:

* **Did blushing stop people liking you? Loving you? Being friends with you?**

* **Would you feel any less about someone who blushed? Or would you feel they were more real?**

* **Even when you have blushed, what actually went wrong?**

* **Even when you felt uncomfortable and thought you may be blushing, what actually happened?**

* **Why would you need to activate your fight-or-flight response (the cause of blushing) in front of those people? Is it not unkind to intimate that they might represent a danger to you?**

* **Is it not unfair to those people that you are accusing them of doing something that will be unpleasant and make you blush? Why does that specific person or people deserve that accusation?**

It is important to also consider the advantages of blushing. For example, dependent on the situation, your blushing may highlight to people your sincere regret if you have made an error. It is a sign that you are human and evidently care. Several studies have suggested that, far from being something to laugh at, the visible reaction of blushing promotes trust and positive judgement in those who see it. It has been shown to make others consider you more approachable and more compassionate.

Blushing is a symptom of a past schema, which you can address and alter as suggested. If you find yourself blushing before you have had a chance to positively condition your schema, take reassurance from the fact that you are showing your friends and colleagues that you understand your mistake, for which they will like and respect you more.

Humour can also help if you find yourself blushing, and the good news is that this is a tool you always have available. Giggling, laughing and smiling helps prevent negative repercussions of blushing in your own mind, and even pretending to laugh or smile helps to stimulate feel-good hormones. Your smile alone can trigger a chemical reaction in the brain, releasing certain hormones such as dopamine and serotonin, which will help to make you feel much better.

Finally . . .

Take a look through your timeline for potential triggers of shyness and blushing, and address them as suggested in this chapter.

With this additional knowledge, consider reflecting on Chapter 3 once more. Have your responses to the self-esteem questionnaire become more positive? Can you add even more positive events and experiences to your timeline? Can you add new friendships and acts of kindness to your timeline? Adding these will help to provide evidence that your shyness or blushing was not as harshly judged by others as you may have previously believed.

Thank you for your help, Nik and Eva.
Feeling empowered and so proud of myself.

Beth

9

Body Confidence

I would just like to thank you. It wasn't totally my choice to come and I had no idea what it involved. I was sceptical of therapy and totally against medication, so I suffered in silence.

Every day I woke up and wished to be someone else.

I loved your advice and it was, for sure, something I could connect with.

After wishing to be someone else I woke up the next day and strangely I was. I have no idea how or why!

I have no idea how you both do this and gain trust, but a huge thank you from my happy heart for your time and energy to make me happy!

Sally

Self-perception

Before reading on, stop for just a moment and take a look in a mirror right now. If there is no mirror available where you are, imagine looking at an image of yourself. How would you describe the person looking back at you? Just pay attention to the words you use about yourself.

Are you using negative, unkind words or, worse still, insulting words and descriptions? Did you compliment yourself at all or manage to see and say anything positive about your body?

If you only used negative words or insults, and were unable to see anything positive, then you are likely suffering with a lack of body confidence.

Most of us will have areas of our bodies that we feel could be improved, but this critique will usually be balanced with something we like about ourselves, or the self-criticism may end with a softening comment such as, 'But I'm not that bad,' or, 'But my partner loves me the way I am,' or, 'But I'm cuddly.'

Synergy

Having body confidence is accepting who you are and how you look, regardless of your weight, age or anything else. Body confidence is also about loving, respecting and accepting yourself physically and emotionally, inside and out. True and absolute confidence is based on a synergy of these thoughts, emotions and feelings.

When you respect and accept the way you look, you carry yourself with confidence, and your body language has a significant impact on your confidence and how others interact with you. Furthermore, self-acceptance and respect will motivate you to be the best you can be physically, mentally and emotionally. True body confidence can also give you the drive, determination and enthusiasm to achieve your goals, whether that is personally or professionally. It gives you confidence, happiness and a more positive outlook, which helps to create stronger bonds, greater respect and relationships with others.

Posture

Your confidence, or lack of it, affects your posture. When you are low in body confidence, you are likely to slouch, avoid eye contact and try to hide or cover up your body. When you feel confident in your body, you will show this in the way you hold yourself, and studies show that this can then affect how other people see you and ultimately deal with you.

A 2009 study at Ohio University found that posture had a significant impact not only on the individual and how they perceived themselves, but also on how they were perceived by others.[21]

The study included seventy-one students who were told they would be taking part in one study, but that part of the study was for the business school and part was for the arts school.

They were told that the arts school was examining the ability to maintain a specific posture while engaging in other activities – the other activity being sitting at a computer and answering questions to investigate job satisfaction and professional performance, which was for the business school.

Some students were told to sit up straight and push their chest out, while others were told to slouch and look towards their knees.

While holding their posture, the students listed either three positive or three negative personal traits relating to future professional performance in a job. After completing this task, the students took a survey in which they rated themselves on how well they would do as a future professional employee.

The results were clear. The upright posture gave the students more confidence in their responses and rating of themselves.

Improving your posture

Positively adjusting your posture will therefore positively influence you, and knowing that posture affects your confidence and body confidence, we would now like you to take a look in a mirror in a seated position, and then again when standing. Take a photograph of yourself in both positions or observe how you look and feel. Score this out of ten.

Now we would like you to repeat this exercise, but with improved posture. Lift and roll your shoulders back. Imagine that a piece of string is attached between the ceiling and the upper centre of your chest, lifting you up. Lift your chin, tuck your pelvis underneath a little and gently bring your abdominal muscles towards your spine. Take a photograph of yourself now, or observe how you look and feel. Score this out of ten. Your improved posture should positively impact how you feel, and how you feel about yourself.

Practise this adjustment often. Put a little note on your computer screen, desk chair, car seat or dining chair to remind yourself to correct your posture to this more confident body position. The more often you do this, the more likely it is to become a new habit.

Low Self-esteem and Body Confidence

People with low self-esteem can often feel unloved, unworthy, insecure, ashamed, pessimistic, unhappy, guilty and very often depressed. This understandably affects confidence and self-belief.

If this is you and sounds familiar, then please consider that how you perceive yourself is largely based upon how other people have made you feel about yourself. Your body confidence issues are therefore likely the result of your self-esteem having been knocked by someone else. Even Kim Kardashian, who is perceived by many to be an incredibly beautiful and strong woman, has said, 'I'm not as sexy as everyone thinks. I am a lot more insecure than people would assume.'

Accepting that no one is born with low confidence or low body confidence is a start to improving and building upon your confidence.

Body Dysmorphic Disorder

Body dysmorphic disorder is a condition that causes obsessive thinking about a supposed physical flaw that is either imagined or hardly noticeable to others. The condition often surfaces during the teenage years, when we are most likely to be concerned with the physical changes of adolescence. Social media can also magnify or contribute to body dysmorphic disorder, by giving opportunities to constantly compare yourself with others. Many people with BDD find themselves compulsively checking their perceived flaw in the mirror or in photographs. It is thought that up to 0.7 per cent of the population suffers from BDD.[22]

Although many individuals may find themselves irritated by a real or imagined physical imperfection, sufferers from BDD are likely to spend hours every day obsessing and worrying about theirs. Some may also find themselves taking excessive measures to 'correct' the flaw, such as surgery.

Sufferers of BDD often feel so repelled or offended by their perceived flaw that they attempt to hide it, or even themselves, from others. In severe cases, BDD can lead to social isolation, depression, self-harm or agoraphobia.

Some people with BDD cannot bear to look at themselves at all, while others are forever looking at themselves in the mirror, obsessing about their looks and feeling distraught at what they see. They will often attempt to find reassurance by pointing out their flaw to others, which can be misconstrued as fishing for compliments.

CASE STUDY
Karlette: Body Dysmorphic Disorder

Karlette had been brutally attacked when she was just fifteen. What started as a playground argument escalated into an out-of-school conflict.

While out shopping one Saturday, a car pulled up and two women jumped out. They started to hit Karlette – first her face, then her ribs. They ripped a chunk of hair from Karlette's scalp while smashing her into a wall, causing a broken cheekbone, fractured ribs and severe bruising to her head.

When we met Karlette she was twenty-two years of age. She had moved away from her hometown soon after the attack and started to self-harm. Karlette's mother told us that her daughter's personality had changed drastically after the attack. Karlette's image had become an obsession. She wouldn't leave the house without a full face of make-up to hide behind, which often took hours to complete.

Karlette told us that, before the attack, she had been studying at a stage school and had wanted to be a TV presenter, but now her confidence was shattered. Her sister joined us, adding that Karlette had gone from being a bubbly, outgoing young teenager to basically a recluse.

It was evident that Karlette had post-traumatic stress disorder, and the attack had also caused her to create body dysmorphic disorder. She believed on some level that she was to blame and had deserved to be attacked. Furthermore, she believed the attack had left her ugly and disfigured. The truth was that the visible scars from the attack had long faded, while her self-inflicted wounds from years of self-harm were now far more visible.

We began therapy by asking Karlette what she saw when she looked in the mirror without make-up on. She said she only saw someone with scars. When we asked what the scars meant to her, she said, 'They make me feel weak.'

She went on to say that she thought one of her eyes had dropped since the attack. We gently explained that she was the only one who could see that – because it was not there, but as a result of what had happened she was unfairly self-punishing. On further discussion and reflection, she agreed and said, 'You're right, I feel a little silly about that now.' Challenging her words and repeating them back to her was helping her to reflect on her self-image schema, which was starting to change for the better.

We asked Karlette if she had been inviting the women who attacked her back into her life over the last seven years to continue their assault. She abruptly said, 'No.'

We then asked who had been attacking her since that day. Karlette thought for a moment and answered, 'Me.' We explained to Karlette that what those girls had done to her was incredibly wrong and that the attack should never have happened. However, we pointed out that the attack had lasted only minutes that one day – yet Karlette had carried on attacking herself for the last seven years.

Karlette was having a deep moment of realisation; we could see her start to sit up straighter, with more confidence. We asked who had done the most damage to her since that day, and she replied, 'Me.'

We reflected on her attack and asked if she deserved to get hurt by two people who were considerably older than her. Karlette said, 'No.'

We asked if what they did was wrong. Karlette said, 'Yes.'

We asked if what she was doing to herself now was wrong. She firmly said 'Yes' again.

We suggested that the attackers had moved on with their lives, yet she hadn't moved on with hers. We showed Karlette a picture of herself taken just after the attack, and pointed out that the image she had been seeing in the mirror for the last seven years was still the same as the one in the photograph. Karlette agreed that she had trapped herself in that moment, with that image. She agreed that it was time to let this image go and allow the girl in the photo to heal. Karlette had carried on from where the girls had left off: they hurt her once, and she had hurt herself every day since.

We wanted Karlette to see what we and everyone else saw – not a beaten-up girl, but a beautiful woman. We removed the photo, revealing a mirror behind it. Karlette looked at herself and smiled. Now, when we asked her to think back to the attack, she revealed that she felt fine – and confused about feeling fine. She began to laugh; at this point we knew she had overcome her PTSD and body dysmorphic disorder.

Some time after therapy, Karlette contacted us to say her confidence had improved so much that she had volunteered for a charity programme, building orphanages in Africa. No make-up required! In 2016, Karlette went on to compete in and win the title of Miss Greater London. She then met her future husband, and she is now very happily married with two children.

> *We accept what we are willing to tolerate. We tolerate what we believe we deserve.*

CASE STUDY
Hannah: Feeling Inadequate

Hannah came to see us, saying that she believed she was compromising her future. She wanted to excel in her career, but her feelings of inadequacy were holding her back. She had worked for the same company for several years, and although she knew she had both the qualifications and experience, she found she was talking herself out of applying for a promotion.

We asked if there was a specific element that she was particularly concerned over, and after a little thought she said the new job would include liaising with clients. When we asked why that might be a worry, Hannah told us that she did not think she looked the part.

We handed Hannah a mirror and asked her what she saw. She responded, 'I see someone drab, pale, plain, boyish, sad, unattractive.' However, to us Hannah was a very beautiful, articulate and intelligent young woman. She told us that she knew the origins of her issues, which she believed arose from the fact that her mum had passed away and her elder sister had left soon after for university, leaving Hannah at home with her father. She described him as being a good provider but unable to give Hannah the attention and clarification of love she needed.

Hannah's questionnaire, and the way she spoke about herself, made it clear that her lack of confidence was based on her belief that she was unattractive. As a result of this we asked Hannah to elaborate a little more about her teenage years.

Hannah shared that her father found a new partner two years or so after her mum had passed away. Around this time Hannah had started high school and found herself getting involved with a group of girls who were, in her words, quite 'superficial' and 'very materialistic'.

When we asked Hannah if these girls had been critical of her or bullied her, she said no, but that they had been very opinionated about everyone else, and would destroy others with their criticism.

We felt it highly likely that the loss of her mum, and not experiencing the love she needed from her father, were contributory factors in Hannah's lack of confidence. But we also needed to address the long-term consequences of her judgemental teen peer group, which were likely signficant.

We began by asking, 'You said your dad did not give you the love you needed, but did he love you?' Hannah said he did.

We asked if she had ever told her dad what her requirements of love were. She confirmed that she had not.

We asked if he had given her any reason to doubt that he loved her. Hannah thought for a little while and said, 'Well, no, but he didn't tell me he loved me either.'

We asked how she thought her dad might have known how to give her what she wanted. Hannah said she was unsure. We asked how her dad knew how to be a dad. Hannah was unsure. We asked, 'Why does your dad have the accent that he does?' Hannah thought for a moment and replied, 'Because of where he came from and his parents.' We went on, 'So how does your dad know how to be a dad?' Hannah then realised that her father's model of a father was most likely based on his own father. She immediately started to defend her own father, saying that her grandfather wasn't very warm and that he had been very strict to her dad growing up.

We asked Hannah, 'What do you think your grandad would consider the necessary requirements for being a good dad?' Hannah responded that it was probably to give you food, a home, clothes, schooling – 'that sort of thing'. We agreed, and explained to Hannah that she was being harsh on her dad, as he had fulfilled *his* criteria for being a loving dad. She could not blame her father for not fulfilling *her* criteria, particularly when she had never told her dad what her needs and expectations were.

Hannah agreed that her dad did love her and had fulfilled everything he believed was necessary. Materially he had given her more than she needed, but he was unaware of her emotional needs so could not be blamed for not fulfilling those.

'Did your dad give you all the love he knew how to give?'
She said, 'Yes.'

We pointed out that Hannah was expecting the love of two parents from just her dad and asked whether this was fair. Hannah said, 'I hadn't considered that.' There was a definite shift in her body language then, as Hannah sighed and relaxed into her seat.

We went on to talk more about the group of girls Hannah socialised with both in and out of school, and asked her to elaborate further on their criticism of others.

Hannah told us that the group, including her, gossiped and bitched about everything and everyone. Their conversations were dominated by boys, make-up, fashion, music and criticising what other girls said, did, wore and looked like. We asked how that had impacted Hannah. How did that make her feel? Had it impacted what she wore? How she looked?

Hannah told us that there was a lot of pressure being in the group, as she felt she always had to look her best. However, despite her efforts, she never felt she was pretty enough, slim enough or good enough. Just as she had helped her group of friends find fault with everyone else, she had become conditioned to find fault with herself, and this was now holding her back by affecting her opinion of herself as an adult, as she anticipated the judgement she had learned at school.

We asked Hannah why she thought the girls in her group were so critical. She felt it was most likely a combination of immaturity, envy of other girls and probably because they had little else going on.

We continued, 'You became sensitive to how you looked as a consequence of your friends. Is that fair to say?' Hannah agreed. 'You criticise yourself now, as your friends did to others, but are you immature and envious, and do you have as little going on as your friends did?' Using Hannah's own words back to her had a great impact, as she responded, 'Of course not.'

We asked whether Hannah's friends were still a part of her life? She confirmed that they had lost touch the moment they had finished high school. We questioned the likelihood of these same girls still judging Hannah. Hannah said, 'There is a zero per cent possibility of them judging me and I honestly don't care what they think of me.'

She suddenly offered the realisation that all the girls, including Hannah, were reliant upon one another but not really compatible as friends. She said, 'We were all girls with a chip on our shoulders, and we deflected our issues by bitching about others, even people that didn't deserve it.'

We asked Hannah whether it was time to stop bitching. 'You've been bitching about yourself, Hannah, and guess what? You don't deserve it either.' Hannah began to cry.

We added gently, 'Hannah, you knew the bitchiest, most critical of girls, yet who did they *not* criticise?'

Hannah thought for a few moments and replied, 'Me.'

We asked, 'Hannah, is it time to grow up and leave the girls and the bitching in the past?'

Hannah responded, 'Definitely.'

We concluded our session with our Mirror Technique (shared later in this chapter, see page 220), which allowed Hannah to see herself through the eyes of love and honesty, and some work on gratitude, also shared later in this chapter (see page 227).

Hannah looked in the mirror again and smiled as she said, 'I look like my mum, and my mum was so pretty.'

Raising Your Body Confidence

It is common to overlook your own qualities and attributes, seeing yourself through a lens of negativity imposed by others, without ever questioning their motives. When you change the way you look at circumstances, the circumstances you look at begin to change, just as they did for Hannah in the case study. It is therefore essential for your confidence to help build your self-esteem, and in so doing your body confidence.

Here are some tips to build your body confidence and address BDD:

* **Look back at your timeline. Did someone at school make you feel bad about yourself? Or perhaps you were envious of someone? Whatever the reason, understanding the origin of your issue will help you to challenge and positively condition it.**

* **If you had a crush on a boy at school who then spurned you, you will undoubtedly have questioned why. If you have a physical feature that you dislike, you might have blamed this as a reason for the rejection. Look for a positive element in the rejection: for example, would you still be interested in that boy today? Childhood crushes rarely last – the rejection might have saved you from wasting your time.**

* **Write a list of all the people who have made you feel bad, who you felt judged you or that you felt you were trying to impress. Were they a school bully, fellow school pupil, parent, teacher, colleague, partner, ex-partner? Now look at the list and consider whether this person or people are still a part of your life. If not, this suggests that you or they have moved on, and therefore you can now sever this emotional tie you have maintained. Just as you have moved on with your life, you now need to decide to move on with your emotions, too.**

* **If anyone on your list is still in your life, consider whether you can distance yourself from them – try the Bungee Technique we shared earlier (see page 124) to alter negative emotional impact by others. If you can't do that,**

tell them how they make you feel – you could write them a letter or speak to them in private.

* If you can't change them, you must change how you deal with and perceive them. For example, if they are very negative to you, try being excessively positive in return. If they criticise you, say something like, 'That was hurtful, but I'll assume you're having a bad day as I know you're too nice to be intentionally mean.' As the same actions create the same results, you must use a different approach to provide a different result.

* Look at the list again, and ask yourself what skills, qualities or qualifications each person has or had to judge you. Why would you choose to allow their views to tarnish your view of yourself?

* Consider what their motive was to say or do the things that hurt you, for example envy or jealousy due to their own insecurities.

* If you ever hear yourself being derogatory to yourself because someone at school said something hurtful (for example, someone called Dave), then when you catch yourself saying those hurtful words to yourself say out loud or in your head, 'Dave, you're not welcome in my life any more.'

* Next, consider whether each person on the list was being kind to you. Unless the situation was a total misunderstanding, they can't possibly have been kind if they made you feel bad. Ask yourself why you would want to carry unkind opinions around with you. If you are speaking to yourself negatively using their words, or as a consequence of their actions, you are reinforcing their

original unkind words and behaviour, which means that you are picking up where they left off. If you see yourself as a kind person, remember that this includes being kind to yourself and therefore being unkind to yourself is not in your nature.

* Are you comparing yourself to others? If so, what do you know about that person's emotional health and strength? Their personal life? Their insecurities?

* Would you ever judge a fish for not being able to climb a tree? Or a butterfly for not being able to swim? This is essentially what you are doing if comparing yourself to someone who is not you. We are all unique, and we each have unique beauty and qualities.

* Have you ever considered that by being negative and disrespectful of who you are, you are also being unkind and disrespectful to your family? Your family tree? Your genetics? You are a combination of all family members who came before you. People who no doubt did – and lived through – remarkable things, and you have inherited so much from them alongside your physical characteristics.

* Would you ever compare yourself to a cartoon character? Or an imaginary figure? Consider that this may be what you are doing in a world of filters and airbrushing. Are you comparing yourself to something that is not real?

* Write a list of everyone who has ever loved you and cared about you a great deal. This can include pets, friends, family and teachers who are either no longer here or are still a part of your life. Was their friendship solely based on how you looked? Would they have stopped loving

or caring for you if you had a bad hair day, gained a few pounds or suddenly had a spot on your face? If not, why not? Why did they love you? Write it down so you can see the evidence of how incredible and loved you are. Realise that if you have ever been loved, this is because you are lovable. Whether the person was or is a parent, sibling, friend or even a pet, consider the reasons why they love or loved you. Write it down. Love is not an emotion that is given freely. It is one that is earned and gifted to those who deserve it. You deserved it.

* At the side of each person on your list, write down at least one reason why that person liked you or a compliment they gave you. See how to deal with compliments later in this chapter (page 226).

I can't believe you have been able to heal me of something that I've struggled with for many years, you truly are fabulous. Thank you!! It was wonderful to meet you.

Rebecca

Mirror Technique

We have used the Mirror Technique with many of the people in the case studies we have shared throughout this book, and at our workshops, and it is an effective way to see yourself through the eyes of love, as you deserve.

We have established that your view of yourself has been based on how others and your life experiences have made you feel. This technique will allow you to get to know yourself, so you can be your own best friend and love yourself just as you have been, are or will be loved by others – unconditionally and with the respect you deserve.

You will need a notepad and pen, a voice recorder on your telephone or a trusted friend to help make notes for you.

Stand in front of a full-length mirror. While looking in the mirror, write down or record everything that you see and say when describing yourself. What kind of person do you see in front of you? Are they weak? Are they strong? What do you look like?

Do you see any weaknesses? If so, what are they?

Write down everything you perceive about yourself. Describe the person standing in front of you, both visually and emotionally. How do you feel about that person?

Look at all your body parts and write down what you see.

Once you have written the list, count how many of those things are negative, and how many of those things that you have said about yourself are positive.

We would now like you to write a list of just the negative things that you have said about yourself. Look at those words and ask yourself, would you ever say those things to a stranger? If not, why not?

The negative things that you have said about yourself, would you ever say them to a friend? If not, why not?

Again, looking at the negative things you have said about yourself, consider whether you would ever say them to your child, partner, parents or a loved one. If not, why not?

Now consider that if you would never say the things you said about yourself to someone you love or to a friend, family member or even to a stranger, this is probably because those words are mean and unkind. Therefore, please consider that, if you are a kind person, and it is not acceptable to say those things to anybody else, then it is absolutely not acceptable to say those things to yourself either.

Now we would like you to look at those negative things you have said about yourself and consider who has said these things to you or who has made you feel this way.

Use the list of confidence saboteurs created in your questionnaire and timeline (see pages 14 and 18). Add anybody else who you feel has contributed to any of the negative, unkind comments that you have said about yourself. Look at that list and ask yourself:

* Why would you want to listen to that person?

* What qualifications did they have to judge you?

* Are they even a part of your life? If not, that is possibly because they are not important to you. However, if they are still a part of your life, then consider why they may have said those things to you.
  • Is it because they were envious or jealous of you?
  • Is it because you have or had something they wanted (e.g. a nice family, nice home, skills, the respect of your teachers, qualities they envied, etc.)?
  • Is it because they were scared of losing you? Therefore, they thought that by knocking your self-esteem, you would be less likely to leave them and find a new friend/partner, and would appreciate them more.
  • Is it because that person felt bad about themselves and in an effort to elevate themselves they had to knock you down?
  • Is it because they feared you would steal their limelight? Maybe from a friend, parent, school teacher, boy or girl they were attracted to?
  • Is it because they were worried that if you became too confident you might leave them or not want them in your life?
  • Is it because they were worried that you may supersede them in life?

Once you have considered these things and realised that those words aren't yours but are based upon somebody else and how they have made you feel, what we would now like you to do is see yourself through the eyes of love, so as to recognise your true inner beauty and value, and to ignite your confidence.

For the next part of the Mirror Technique, use a telephone with a voice-recording option or a tape recorder if you have one – this is the most effective way to do the exercise as it is far more beneficial if you can keep your eyes closed. If not, then keep your eyes closed and write down everything positive that you can remember once you have actually completed the next part of the technique.

Stand in front of the mirror and close your eyes. If you are a little bit unsteady, you may want to get a chair to put to the side of you to give you something to hold onto – or sit on the chair if you are unable to stand.

With your eyes closed, think of someone who loves you unconditionally now or who has in the past. That may be a partner, a parent, a best friend, a colleague, a school teacher, a pet or someone who has even passed away, such as a grandparent. However, just think of somebody who has or does love you unconditionally.

Still with your eyes closed, imagine that person standing to the side of you. As you picture them standing to the side of you, shoulder to shoulder, imagine that you are floating out of your body and into that person's body, and then looking through their eyes at your reflection in the mirror.

What we would now like you to do – and hopefully you can record this – is to say out loud all the things that person sees or saw in you. So, looking through your loved one's eyes at your reflection in the mirror, say out loud what that person loves about you: what do they see? How do they describe you? Why do they say they love you?

For example:

* **Do they tell you that they love you?**

* **Do they say you are beautiful, kind, intelligent, fun to be around? That you are loyal, that you are perfect, that you are a good cook, a good housekeeper, good at doing something in particular? That you are good at making them feel special or loved?**

* **What do they say about your looks? Do they or did they compliment your hair, eyes, figure, stature, dress sense or smile?**

Now, knowing that the person who loves or loved you is not a liar, and therefore their feelings towards you are honest and true, say out loud all the compliments that person has ever said about you and everything they love about you while imagining your reflection. Say it as they said it, while imagining that you are looking through your loved one's eyes, and repeat their words four or five times with the love, sincerity and meaning they gifted to you.

Alternatively, use your recording. Press play and, with your eyes closed again, imagine seeing yourself in the mirror through the eyes of your loved one, imagine your reflection in that mirror and listen to all the words that person said about you, everything that person loves about you. Repeat this four or five times.

If you can't do this with a voice recording, that is absolutely fine – just remember to say out loud all the compliments and all the things that this person feels, says and has ever thought about you. Keep repeating the kind words with meaning, over and over, four or five times.

Once you have done this and said or heard on your recording all the lovely things that this person has ever said or felt about you, very slowly open your eyes and see yourself for the first time in that mirror through the eyes of love.

See yourself, knowing that the person who said all those lovely things about you said them because they were true and accepting that people do not give compliments without reason.

People do not give love without reason. Love is earned, and if anyone has ever loved or does love you unconditionally, this is because *you* have earned it and it is because you are lovable.

Now write down all those compliments and positive things that your loved one said about you, felt about you and sees in you. Keep them somewhere prominent. This could be at the side of your bed, on the sun visor in your car, in your desk at work, in your bag or wallet, on the refrigerator door or in all these places. Look at them regularly, and whenever you need to remind yourself of how amazing you are, how loved you are and that you deserve to be happy, healthy and confident, reread this list and hear your loved one's voice as you read it.

Finally, return to your timeline, look at your positive list and consider each entry, then consider any positives you might have overlooked or forgotten to add, such as a time when you laughed uncontrollably, a time when you fell in love, whether with a person, place or pet, a time when you were given a compliment or achieved something, a place you visited or a memorable experience, such as a party or a day out. Now you can invest in yourself by reading this list often and reminding yourself of how incredible and fabulous you are, and of all the wonderful things you have seen, experienced, tried or been a part of.

Thank you for such an amazing day. I can't believe how I feel! I feel so real and beautiful. xxxxx

Anna

Techniques to Aid Your Body Confidence

Accept compliments

We often dismiss or shrug off a compliment. You may have been told how well you look and your response is, 'Oh, I feel awful, I've gained weight,' or someone compliments your T-shirt and you default to, 'This old thing.' However, do not underestimate the therapeutic benefits of accepting a compliment. Every time you bat away a compliment, you are nurturing your lack of body confidence and low self-esteem. However, consider a compliment for what it is. A compliment is a gift, and to bat off or dismiss it is like giving a gift back to the recipient, which is impolite and unfair.

The great news is that the resolution to this issue is simple, and something that you have done many times before. To start building your self-worth and body confidence, whenever someone gives you a compliment simply say, 'Thank you.' Yes, that's it: 'Thank you!' You have said those words many, many times before and therefore you shouldn't find it difficult. It may feel a little strange to begin with, but saying thank you is the courteous and most positive response for both you and the person gifting you with their kind words.

Positive points

Consider three things you like about yourself or that someone you love or trust has complimented you on. Write the compliments on an index card or Post-it note and stick it on your alarm clock or mirror, then say them out loud every morning from today.

If you find yourself doubting these compliments or responding to yourself with something negative, remind yourself that this is unkind and rude. If this were a compliment given to you by someone else, then realise that you would effectively be calling them a liar, and that is unfair.

Gratitude

If you suffer with body dysmorphic disorder or a low level of body confidence, it is likely that you use derogatory terms about your body or certain body parts when speaking both to yourself and others. This is like bullying each body part, which only makes you feel worse. We would like you to change this inner dialogue by showing your body some gratitude instead.

For example, instead of saying, 'I hate my thighs,' ask yourself: 'What do my thighs allow me to do?' Try saying something positive, like, 'I am grateful to my thighs, as they enable me to ride my bike, move anywhere I want and also run outside.'

Here are some more examples:

'I hate my nose.'
'I am grateful to my nose, as it helps me to smell my perfume.'

'I hate that scar.'
'I am grateful to that scar, because it is a sign that I survived.'

'I hate my bum.'
'I am grateful to my bum, because it makes sitting down very comfortable.'

Don't fuel the fire

Do not cultivate or encourage self-criticism by interacting with friends who are judgemental of others or who have low body confidence themselves and frequently berate their bodies or body image. This will fuel the fire of your own self-criticism and make it harder for you to feel positive. Learn that this is not a helpful way to speak about yourself, or for your friends to speak about themselves or others. Learn to break the habit by politely and supportively declining to join in. If you find yourself in this situation with a friend who is critiquing their supposed physical flaws, try countering every negative they throw out with a positive. We love the phrase 'but luckily . . .'

They say: 'I've put on so much weight.'

You say: 'But luckily your boyfriend loves you the way you are.'

They say: 'I look terrible.'

You say: 'But luckily I don't see that.'

They say: 'My bum looks so fat.'

You say: 'But luckily you still look great in those jeans.'

Treat yourself

Giving your body a treat can help you to feel better. Massage is a great way to learn to take pleasure in your own body, has been shown to boost overall self-confidence and helps you connect to yourself. When was the last time you treated your body with care and attention instead of berating it?

You may think you don't like your body, but showing it some love and respect could help you love and respect your body more. This can be something simple, such as a weekly home body scrub, followed by deep moisturising, or you could treat yourself to an occasional massage or facial at a salon or spa. If you are enjoying a facial or massage, why not thank those body parts for making the experience so pleasurable?

Don't let marketing blind you to your own beauty

Our world is awash with advertising. In order to encourage us to become consumers, we are fed a media diet of what we could, should and must look like. This barrage of marketing suggests that we are not good enough as we are, in order to prompt us to buy, buy, buy! We are told that we need to be slimmer, prettier, younger and happier in order to be fulfilled, and this leads us to make negative comparisons between ourselves and what we see on the television or in magazines.

Firstly, we must appreciate that we are being manipulated to encourage us to buy a product. Secondly, if you find yourself comparing yourself to others, you are wasting your time and energy focusing on other people's lives rather than your own.

> **Comparing one's body to those of individuals perceived as more attractive is common among college women, and has been associated with increases in body dissatisfaction.**
> **Emilie Pinkasavage et al., 2015**[23]

The truth is, you will never be anyone but yourself. The Mirror Technique shared in this chapter (see page 220) will help you truly value your qualities. You are unique and therefore perfect as you are. Your beauty, happiness, success and body confidence come from your thoughts, actions, gratitude and appreciation of who you are, NOT your looks or figure.

I've changed so much. Nik and Eva have been FABULOUS on social media, keeping in touch, and I cannot praise such wonderful people enough.

Danielle

WOW List

The positive list you created during the Mirror Technique, together with the positives on your timeline, can now start to make up your WOW List – a list of everything that is 'wow' and exceptional about you.

Why allow chance to predict your mood when you wake up in the morning? Having your WOW List by the side of your bed is a great way to end and start your day, to remind you how wonderful you are the way you are. It will help you take on your day ahead with confidence.

Just as working out physically will make you stronger and healthier, exercises such as the WOW List and your positive list will help to develop your confidence and self-love. This growth will then become habitual, so stick with it and enjoy celebrating the person you are.

Thank you so much to Nik and Eva for such an inspiring and life-changing day. Thank you for sharing your knowledge, passion and kindness with everyone.
You are two very beautiful people.
Much love x

Lucy

Celebrity comparison

If you feel insecure about your own body, you may compare yourself unfavourably to a celebrity who you believe is naturally slim or happy in their body, with their seemingly perfect figure, perfect skin and perfect life. But as we have established, you aren't a mind reader. No matter how perfect this person appears on the outside, it is impossible for you to know how they feel on the inside.

There have been numerous celebrities who, in a frenzy of press, have claimed they've lost weight and never felt happier. Others have claimed to be happy being overweight, only to lose weight and then claim they were never happy being big. We see people who we believe are perfect, who then admit to having depression, or worse, tragically take their own life. Hugely successful people will admit to a drug or alcohol problem due to grave inner unhappiness.

Longing to be someone else is an impossible dream that will only lead to misery. Learning to see and celebrate your own unique attributes and qualities is an achievable dream worth chasing.

We hope that this chapter and the exercises shared, coupled with the Mirror Technique (see page 220), will allow you to see the beautiful and remarkable person that you are in this moment – and will always be.

> *Don't compare yourself to others. Just as no one can play your role better than you, you can't play their role better than them.*

10

Eating Disorders

Fantastic day . . . Thank you . . . I don't have to change.
The people that matter love me exactly how I am.

Carrie

In this chapter we would like to share with you some of the consequences of low self-esteem in relation to overeating and undereating.

The NHS defines an eating disorder as 'when you have an unhealthy attitude to food, which can take over your life and make you ill'.[24] Eating disorders can take many forms, but the most well known are anorexia nervosa (restricting food intake, resulting in severe weight loss), bulimia (binge eating followed by purges, either through vomiting, laxatives or excessive exercise) and binge-eating disorder (BED), in which individuals consume excessive amounts of food beyond the point of hunger.

Quite surprisingly, at the time of writing, obesity is not incorporated into the range of classified 'eating disorders', yet obesity appears to fall into the aforementioned criteria of an 'unhealthy attitude to food, which can take over your life and make you ill', as stipulated by the NHS. Although for some obesity can be a consequence of an illness, certain medications or perhaps poor knowledge of how to eat healthily, for many overeating is a consequence of a past or present emotional pain.

In our opinion, regardless of an official diagnosis, if you obsess about eating or not eating, if you struggle to eat the way others do, if you restrict your food or binge, then you may suffer from disordered eating. These distressing issues with food may be a consequence of low confidence, or they may contribute to your feelings of low self-esteem.

Self-medicating

Eating disorders are most often a consequence of underlying thoughts and feelings. The eating disorder may be a way of coping, self-medicating, self-sabotaging or self-harming, or it may act as something to hide behind or, in some cases, a way of trying to feel in control.

Eating disorders and confidence issues are often self-perpetuating, as having an eating disorder may magnify a confidence issue, making someone who previously had manageable lack of confidence develop an extreme lack of confidence because of how they believe they look. This lack of confidence can be compounded by guilt or shame for having succumbed to an eating disorder.

Equally, low self-esteem and a lack of confidence can lead to negative feelings such as anxiety, shame, regret, frustration and insecurity, which can go on to promote and develop an eating disorder.

Rather than undertaking therapy or self-development for these feelings of anxiety and insecurity, or for difficulties handling testing circumstances, many people will look for a simple and accessible remedy, distraction or short-term fix. Some people will obtain medication from their doctor, but many will look to self-medicate in some form, often meaning they turn to, or away from, food.

The food we enjoy helps to release feel-good hormones to boost our mood. As endorphins are released, this causes the pulse to speed up and provides a good feeling, similar to when you fall in love. If we experience painful emotions, we may turn to food as a short-term boost or distraction, and often this will be junk food.

The desire to self-medicate can be a consequence of feeling undervalued or not good enough, which often originates from prior bullying, humiliation or being mistreated. This can then lead to self-sabotaging, when you believe you don't deserve to look good or feel good.

Overeating and Junk Food

We've all seen movies where the heartbroken heroine sits on the sofa with a tub of ice cream to soothe her heartbreak. This isn't just a movie cliché but a coping mechanism, because sweet, fatty, processed junk foods have a significant effect on the reward area of the brain.

Junk food triggers the pleasure centres of the brain and releases the feel-good chemicals dopamine and serotonin. Feel-good neurotransmitters such as dopamine can be rapidly released, causing us to feel as if our problems are less worrying.

It is important to understand that food addiction is not caused because you are greedy, or because you have no willpower, but more because you feel you need the short-term feel-good effects the junk food provides. It is therefore vital to address the cause of your low feelings, rather than trying to smother them with food. Overeating to excess can cause you to feel worse in the long run.

We suggest turning to your timeline to try to identify a moment, perhaps in your childhood, when you may have turned to food to cope with difficult feelings. Did your parents try to stop you crying by giving you sweets? Did you find it hard to get anyone to listen to your difficulties?

Common Causes of Eating Disorders

Past unresolved emotional issues

It is possible that you may be self-medicating as a result of past unresolved issues, which have gone on to cause negative feelings and emotions. These unresolved issues, such as bullying, abuse, neglect, confusion, guilt, shame or low self-esteem, can then negatively impact your confidence.

Reward

You may find yourself using junk food to rekindle the comfort and positive emotions from childhood, when foods such as chocolate and sweets were given as a reward, treat or celebration. Certain foods, therefore, can lead to positive emotional associations later in life, which you may seek at times when you are feeling low. This may be relevant to you if you feel disappointment or sadness at not having been able to achieve something due to your lack of confidence.

Tiredness, exhaustion and insomnia

If your sleep is affected due to regret, self-criticism or persistently replaying something you did or said that you believed was incorrect, then you may find you turn to food for a quick pick-me-up. Poor sleep causes lack of energy and tiredness, and an increased release of the hormone ghrelin, which creates feelings of hunger. This combination of factors explains why a night of poor sleep can lead to cravings for sugars and simple carbohydrates to provide a quick boost of energy.

Depression

When feeling low, junk food can become a go-to. It is an easily accessible form of temporary self-medication to help ease feelings in the moment, both as a distraction and by offering the benefits of dopamine and serotonin release, which helps temporarily elevate mood.

Low self-esteem

In addition to temporarily elevating mood, junk food can also be used as a tool to unconsciously self-sabotage or self-punish for past life events. These could include times when you were made to feel inadequate or worthless. Equally, some people may go on to gain weight as a form of protection, particularly if lacking confidence, so as to feel less attractive and therefore not encourage attention from people – particularly a possible love interest. This self-protection is often an unconscious reaction, which is why the timeline shared at the start of this book is such an important and effective tool in dealing with all past schemas, some of which you may not have been aware of.

Heartache or loneliness

For people who lack confidence in social situations, eating or drinking can help to offer a distraction when lonely, thanks to the brief elevated mood they provide.

Substance abuse

Junk food can satisfy the artificial urge to eat created by other forms of self-medication, such as alcohol, drugs or the come-down from both.

Void filler

Eating or drinking alcohol can be a distraction, and will often help to fill a void, particularly when lonely or if we have too much time on our hands.

Stress, anxiety or upset

For those unsure how to deal with daily issues, problems, upsets and anxieties, junk food can offer a quick, easy and accessible element of temporary relief or distraction.

> **'Happiness is when what you think, what you say and what you do are in harmony.'**
>
> **Gandhi**

CASE STUDY
Kelly: Not Feeling Good Enough

Kelly was the eldest of five girls. She told us that she had lovely memories from her first six years when she was the only child, receiving her mum's full and constant attention. However, having had four more children in relatively quick succession, as each sister was born, Kelly felt that she was moving further and further away from her mum.

As a child, Kelly had identified that she would receive her mum's attention and praise if she carried out tasks to help, thus she created a learning or schema that *to receive love and attention, I have to do tasks for others*. She believed she could only be valued by pleasing others.

As the years went on, because Kelly had created the behavioural schema that she had to do things for others in order to obtain love and attention, she became completely subservient and overly eager to please. Kelly was the one at school who would offer to help the teachers, she would stay behind after class if anything needed to be done, she would do things for her friends and, sadly, on occasion she would be taken for granted.

Kelly was also struggling with her weight throughout her childhood, developing an unhealthy relationship with food. She married when she was twenty-two and had two children. As a people pleaser, she would insist on doing everything for her husband and children, yet she was quietly resentful that no one did anything for her. Her difficulties with food continued.

Kelly confirmed that during the times when she felt she was getting love and attention, such as when she first met her husband, when they were first married and when they had the children, she was able to control her eating far better.

We also identified that during times when Kelly felt undervalued, any diets she may have been on would come to an abrupt end and her overeating behaviours would kick in.

Identifying this pattern was a huge breakthrough moment for Kelly. Her lack of understanding of her behaviour with food and yo-yo dieting had made her feel like a failure, and subsequently feel bad about herself. We helped Kelly to change her perspective of childhood events that we felt were contributing to her low self-esteem and yo-yo dieting.

We began by asking her, as a mum of two children, whether she loved her elder child less than her second? Kelly immediately said no. We went on to ask Kelly whether her love for her elder child diminished in any way once her second child arrived? Kelly said she adored both of her children equally.

Furthermore, when we pointed it out, Kelly agreed that, like her own mum, once her new baby arrived her attention was given more to the younger child, who was less capable.

She confirmed that this was never because of favouritism.

For the first time, Kelly had allowed herself to see the situation for what it was, and not how it had felt to a six-year-old little girl. Kelly cried. She went on to say that she felt a little silly that she had not really seen this before. It was now clear to Kelly that her mum's lack of attention did not mean she loved her any less.

We then looked at Kelly's eagerness to please people. It appeared that she, like many, was willing to do far more for others than for herself, and often to her own detriment. However, as Kelly had a schema that 'doing things for others meant love', she expected others to do the same for her in return, and when they did not, she misinterpreted this as meaning that *she* 'wasn't good enough'.

To help positively condition this inaccurate and negative schema we asked Kelly to consider how often she actually allowed people to do things for her. We asked her, if there was a task to be done, would she even let anybody else undertake that task? She thought about this and realised that she was her own worst enemy. In reality, she never allowed this to happen. In fact, she was often depriving someone else of the satisfaction of conducting an act of kindness towards her. Furthermore, although she felt taken for granted, she realised that she had never asked her family for help either.

Finally, living in a home of five children, competition existed when it came to food. Kelly knew that if there were treats in the house and she didn't get to them and eat them quickly, then her sisters would. Therefore, she also created a schema that '*if I don't eat what is available quickly, I will miss out*'. We helped Kelly overcome this by helping her understand why she had created this learning and reminding her that she no longer lived with her sisters, and therefore this schema was no longer relevant or necessary.

Four months later, Kelly updated us to say that the extreme desire to eat sweet foods had gone. A year later, Kelly contacted us again and shared an unexpected positive progression in her life. Kelly said healthy eating, weight loss and exercising was making her feel stronger and happier emotionally and physically. She said that she had also noticed a positive change in the dynamics of her relationship with her husband. As she was changing, her husband had, too; he had become progressively more attentive towards her.

CASE STUDY
Jackie: Self-medicating

When Jackie walked into our health club nearly twenty years ago, it appeared as if she did not want anyone to see or look at her, and she felt very uncomfortable. Back then, Jackie was a UK size 24 (US size 20), and when we sat and spoke with her at length, as we did with all our members, she started to tell us that she desperately needed to make changes in her life.

She was a mum of five children, she worked in a canteen serving food in a male-orientated industry, and she had very low self-esteem and absolutely no confidence.

As the weeks went by and we got to know her, she started to tell us a little bit more about her life. It transpired that Jackie was in a violent and abusive marriage. She was often spoken down to and made to feel worthless and inadequate. She stayed because she didn't think she was capable of managing on her own with five children. She also went on to tell us that at work, although she knew it wasn't done out of malice, the men she served would often tease her because of her size. When coming into the canteen they would say things such as, 'Hope there is some food left and Jackie hasn't eaten all the pies.'

Obviously, coupled with how she was being made to feel at home, what her colleagues perceived as 'fun banter' was not only very hurtful, but further destroying Jackie's confidence and self-esteem.

Thankfully, with the encouragement of our team, Jackie decided that she was worth the investment in herself and joined our health club. We explained to Jackie the importance of understanding her eating patterns, and asked her to complete a food diary for us. It was evident that her eating was far worse just before lunchtimes during the working week and in the evenings. Together, we addressed what the common denominator might be with those specific days of the week. Jackie had a lightbulb moment. From her morning break at work, as lunchtime approached, she started to snack, and when discussing her thoughts and feelings around that time, Jackie was absolutely sure this was to 'cheer herself up' as she dreaded the lunch shift, when she would have to fake a smile in response to all the cutting comments.

The commonality with evenings was that this was when her husband would go to the pub, after which he would most often come home drunk and be aggressive towards her. It was clear that Jackie was self-medicating with food. She felt bad, and food was helping to offer a brief moment of comfort and respite.

Over several months we worked with Jackie, not just on her fitness and nutritional plan, but also helping her to understand the concept of why people become bullies, which was important for Jackie's recovery from self-medicating with food. Jackie did not deserve to be treated as she was; she needed to see and accept that she was without blame, and that there was no truth in the things that were being said to her.

We started to see a real change in Jackie. She was losing weight and becoming more confident, and it was a pleasure to watch her walk into the health club with her head held high and her shoulders back.

Over twelve months, Jackie went from a UK size 24 to a size 14 (US size 10), and one day, very proudly and confidently, she told us that she had left her husband at last. He had come home drunk and started getting violent. For the first time she stood up to him and said, 'If you ever hit me again, it's over!' The day after he did, and she told him to leave.

Because Jackie had taken control of her health and was actually putting herself first, she was starting to flourish, gain confidence and become the person she was supposed to be.

Jackie's life went on to change in numerous ways. She left her job, then met and married somebody who loved and respected her.

Restriction and Undereating

I was anorexic since the age of ten, so for eight years. I had a huge fear of food in general [and] getting fat instantly. It was so ridiculous, but seemed real. I was seriously underweight.

My mum tried everything in her power to make me eat. She would shout at me, and it was an ongoing fight. My dad had to come home from Singapore, and there was a frantic rush to find a treatment centre.

They took me to hospital and said you're going to die if you don't eat, but I was like I don't care. I felt really bad, knowing that my parents had spent over £100,000, but it just didn't work for me. I felt purposeless. My illness stopped me doing anything.

Since having three sessions with Nik and Eva, I stopped concentrating on what I was eating and how many calories I was burning, and a year on life is just so much better. I'm out with the rest of the world doing what everyone else is doing, and life is just so much better. I've got my life back and I can't thank Nik and Eva enough, I'm so grateful.

Sophie B.

Anorexia nervosa

Anorexia nervosa is a condition that results in the person not eating enough, often exercising too much and obsessing about weight. Sufferers also have a distorted image of their body, believing that they are fat when they are actually too thin and underweight, at a detriment to their health.

Anorexia is a dangerous and distressing illness, both for the sufferer and their family, and requires prompt specialist help and support. The sooner the condition is identified and medical help sought, the better.

Anorexia can be life-threatening, and has the highest mortality rate of any mental disorder. Famous actress and singer Demi Lovato once suffered with both anorexia and bulimia. She said in an interview that she didn't think she would make it to twenty-one.

We would urge anyone struggling with anorexia to speak with their doctor, a therapist, a counsellor or a specialist eating disorder charity that can provide help and support. Be aware that, like all eating disorders, anorexia is also a symptom, behind which lies a cause.

Causes of anorexia can vary. Some that we have encountered in our clinic have included bullying, relationship issues, a volatile home life, parents splitting up, exclusion from a group, wanting to belong to a group, feeling invisible and commonly needing to feel in control of something as a result of feeling out of control in life.

Realistically, there is no quick fix for anorexia and recovery is a journey. In addition to the cause being dealt with, confidence has to be worked on, a family support network is essential and the desire of the sufferer to participate in their recovery is paramount. However, hope and help are available, and doctors are incredibly caring and sympathetic, therefore it is essential to seek medical advice and help. If approaching medical professionals feels too difficult, start by speaking to someone you love or trust.

CASE STUDY
Melody: Anorexia

Melody was an incredibly beautiful young woman who came to see us with her mother. They both looked broken by Melody's anorexia, as if they had hit a threshold and did not know where else to turn. Melody's mum cried as she shared the years of therapy and residential establishments Melody had attended. She felt she had let her daughter down, and that she must somehow be responsible for Melody's condition.

As Melody's mum left so that we could start our therapy session, we felt such sadness for a fellow parent, so visibly helpless and emotionally broken.

We knew years of residential care and therapy could make Melody guarded, so knew we had to try a different approach to what she had endured before. Instead of trying to tell her how important it was to eat, we simply asked her, 'Why did you need to go on hunger strike?'

Looking through the timeline and questionnaire that we had asked Melody to complete, we noted that just prior to her eating disorder taking hold, Melody experienced a cluster of events that had proved confusing and traumatic for her.

Having always been a high achiever in her lessons, a grade-A student, Melody had always felt confident and content academically. Having made it to the private school she now attended, for the first time Melody was made to feel, in her words, 'substandard'. She now started to feel insecure and had lost her confidence. Furthermore, the group of girls she hung out with were cutting, opinionated and from fairly wealthy backgrounds, and Melody felt like 'the poor girl' of the group, as she was unable to compete in the fashion and beauty stakes with her friends.

Melody had gone from never really paying much attention to how she looked and what she wore, to feeling that her appearance was a possible target for ridicule and embarrassment. Melody admitted that her friends would target anyone who they believed to be fat, ugly or 'a nerd', and she felt bad that she hadn't stopped them. This made her feel embarrassed and ashamed.

To start to build on her self-esteem, we explained to Melody a little about human behaviour, explaining that survival was our most paramount primal instinct. Melody kept quiet to survive, not to be unkind. We asked what the repercussions might have been had she challenged her friends. Melody responded that she would have likely been excluded from the group. We asked, even if she were excluded from the group, would her speaking out have made any difference to their behaviour? Melody confirmed it would not. We saw Melody's shoulders drop and soften at this realisation, as a glimmer of positive self-acceptance was evident.

We asked Melody, 'Do you accept that your self-awareness about how you look is as a consequence of the girls from school?' Melody agreed.

We repeated, 'Melody, you said your friends were bullies. They were "mean girls" who would also target anyone they believed to be fat, ugly or "a nerd", so why then did they not target and bully you?'

Melody did not speak for some time as the question began to sink in. We repeated the question and Melody began to answer.

What started as a whisper soon became easier for Melody to say out loud: 'Because they liked me.' We gently pushed a little more: 'And knowing they would target anyone they believed to be fat or ugly, why did they not target you?' Eventually Melody said: 'They mustn't have thought I was fat or ugly.'

This was a huge breakthrough.

Now Melody could accept that her friends can't have deemed her as fat or ugly, in a subsequent therapy session we asked Melody to consider whether those same friends were judging her now on how she looked? She confirmed that all the girls were no longer a part of her life.

To help Melody appreciate herself, we looked through her timeline. The positives she had written were minimal, so together we helped her consider more positive memories as we gently encouraged her to share academic achievements, acts of kindness, fun holidays, and times of celebration and laughter to build her self-esteem.

Together we also wrote a list of all the people that she loved and those who had loved her. Questioning the intellect and integrity of each person allowed Melody to accept that these people were not liars, helping her to accept that she had earned their love, because they saw something lovable in her.

We knew that Melody still had a journey ahead, but we helped her to seek health, and to acknowledge that the people in her life – even her group of school friends – had all cared about her and wanted her in their lives, even before she lost weight. We encouraged Melody to find hobbies and interests that excited her to help occupy her thoughts more productively, and to show gratitude to her parents for her life and lifestyle, and to trust them to aid her on her recovery to good health.

Now in her late twenties, Melody has attended many of our workshops, and it is always such a delight to see the healthy, happy young woman that she has become. The last time we saw her, she told us that she was soon to move in to her first home with her fiancé.

> *To change the behaviour resulting from a behavioural schema, the behavioural schema has to be changed.*

Bulimia

People who have bulimia go through periods where they binge eat a large quantity of food in a very short space of time, often when feeling low. In an effort to rid themselves of what they have consumed and the calories, many will then make themselves sick, with other bulimics also using laxatives, excessive exercise, or a combination of all these things to prevent themselves from gaining weight.

After a binge, the individual may feel guilty, fat, anxious and sad. Bulimia often goes hand in hand with low self-esteem. Because the eating disorder is less likely to result in extreme weight loss than anorexia, many sufferers may appear outwardly healthy and successful. Famous faces who have openly spoken about their battle with bulimia have included Paula Abdul, Russell Brand and Princess Diana.

There are numerous health implications associated with bulimia, which can include an irregular menstrual cycle or no cycle at all, a sore throat from vomiting, tooth decay as a consequence of stomach acids affecting tooth enamel, heart disease and a host of bowel-related issues if abusing laxatives.

I have been suffering with my body image, low self-esteem and complete obsession with my weight, exercise and over the last couple of years laxative abuse. You have given [me] the tools I need. I have stopped taking laxatives, and have thrown away the weighing scales. I feel wonderful and grateful . . . and now I feel fantastic.

Mikki S.

CASE STUDY
Isabella: Bulimia

Isabella had come to the UK as a student from Eastern Europe and was living with an English family, Adrian, Terri and their children. Terri was becoming increasingly concerned with Isabella's eating habits.

Terri had noticed that Isabella went to the bathroom for a prolonged length of time after family meals. This concerned Terri, who consequently developed a heightened awareness of everything Isabella did around food. She noticed discarded shopping receipts in the waste bin confirming purchases of laxatives and large quantities of junk food, yet Isabella was thin. She also noticed that Isabella had bought some scales to weigh herself.

Unsure how to approach Isabella with their concerns and not wishing to upset her, Terri booked one of our workshops and decided to bring Isabella along, hoping to pass it off as a 'treat' and that if there were an issue, perhaps it might help.

During our workshop, we spoke about confidence and self-esteem, and how many people struggle with both, often as a consequence of having been bullied or made to feel inadequate at some time in their life. We went on to touch on the possible consequences of these negative life events, which included eating disorders such as anorexia, bulimia, binge eating and overeating. Unbeknown to us, our words were touching a nerve with Isabella, and when we asked for a volunteer for us to demonstrate our confidence-building technique, she bravely raised her hand.

As she joined us on the stage, Isabella told us how she felt she lacked love as a child growing up. As a consequence she had quickly immersed herself in a relationship with a young man at college, giving him every ounce of her attention and time. She explained that he had become aggressive and possessive, and made her feel she was fat, stupid and useless.

As we asked Isabella to look in the mirror on our stage and describe what she saw, she used degrading, disrespectful words about herself. We later asked how many of the words she was using to describe herself had been based on the words of her ex-boyfriend or how he had made her feel. Isabella cried as she confirmed 'most of them'.

We helped Isabella to see herself through the eyes of love and to realise and appreciate her true worth.

We asked her to consider any possible motive her ex may have had to destroy her self-esteem. Isabella shared how all his previous girlfriends had cheated on him, and that perhaps he was punishing her for their mistakes. We pointed out that cheating girlfriends would have knocked his confidence. This made his behaviour towards Isabella more about his own issues than hers: he was trying to make her feel bad about herself so that she would feel lucky to have him as a boyfriend, making her less likely to stray.

This resonated with Isabella, and she accepted that she was a beautiful and kind person, both inside and out, and that in hindsight her ex's fear of losing her proved he must have felt she was too good for him.

Isabella walked off stage to an enormous round of applause, with her shoulders back and head held high. At the end of the workshop, Terri made her way over to speak with us. She explained to us why she had brought Isabella to the workshop and about her suspicions. She also told us that after she had come off stage, Isabella had hugged Terri and thanked her, and at the next break she admitted to Terri that she had been, in her words, 'self-harming', using laxatives and making herself sick. She felt that she was fat and ugly, which made her want to eat junk food, after which she would feel disgusted with herself and then make herself sick. Isabella told Terri that she felt lighter and happier from the workshop experience.

> *If the cause is the foundation, the symptom is the structure. If the foundation is removed, the structure falls down.*

Other specified feeding or eating disorder (OSFED)

Some conditions that fall into the category of 'Other specified feeding or eating disorders' include:

Night-eating syndrome

Night-eating syndrome is very common and is where someone eats a lot of food after their evening meal or wakes up from sleep to eat. Many people with NES feel like they have no control and often feel ashamed or guilty the next morning, with good intentions for the new day ahead, which they rarely manage to see through. People with NES often consume the majority of their daily calorific intake after their evening meal. Common causes of NES include not eating regularly through the day, overly restricted daytime food intake, lack of good-quality sleep, loneliness, boredom, tiredness, stress or unresolved emotional issues, including lack of confidence and low self-esteem.

Purging disorder

People with purging disorder try to influence their weight or body shape by using laxatives, diuretics, excessive exercise or fasting, but they do not binge. It is believed that purging mainly affects women, with up to 70 per cent of sufferers also having a mood disorder, and up to 43 per cent having an anxiety disorder.[25]

People who purge have similar feelings to those who suffer with bulimia or binge-eating disorder, and often feel guilt and shame, and therefore do not always admit they have a problem or ask for help, which of course they should.

Binge-eating disorder

Binge eating is probably a condition that many people who struggle with weight and overeating issues can relate to, as many of us have 'binge eaten' at some time. Binge eating is when a person eats a large amount of food – often unhealthy food – beyond the point of hunger. It is often the consequence of unresolved emotional issues.

If you experience binge-eating disorder, you might be using food to help make you feel better: to cheer you up, to fill a void, to distract you, to comfort you or even to provide company when feeling lonely.

In our experience, binge-eating disorder often goes hand in hand with people who are stressed, anxious, have low self-esteem or who have faced numerous life challenges.

Binge eaters feel out of control with their eating, and therefore often feel ashamed and embarrassed. This shame may prevent sufferers from seeking help, but there can be numerous negative physical and health consequences with binge-eating disorder, such as weight gain, diabetes and high blood pressure. It is important to recognise that any way of eating that affects your health is a sign of an underlying issue, and it should be addressed rather than ignored.

Overcoming Eating Disorders That Affect Your Confidence

The caterpillar has become the butterfly finally. I'm so grateful.

Emma

If your eating disorder is a consequence of lack of confidence and low self-esteem, and is creating these negative behaviours, the most effective formula for combatting it is:

1 Address the cause.

2 Understand your eating patterns and triggers.

3 Use techniques such as distraction to negate your triggers.

4 Build your confidence.

5 Drink plenty of water.

6 Eat healthily and make sure you get enough sleep.

7 Adopt an exercise routine.

8 Consider confiding in a loved one or a health professional.

1 Address the cause

As you now no doubt understand, your lack of confidence was not something you were born with. A cause for your eating disorder exists, and this is why it is essential to look through your timeline to consider possible events that made you feel undervalued, embarrassed, ashamed, useless, worthless, foolish, etc. The question you are looking to answer is: 'Who and what event made me doubt myself?' Things to consider include:

* **Have you ever been bullied? A recent survey found that there is a link between young people who were bullied going on to develop an eating disorder.**

* **Has anyone ever made you feel inferior or worthless, or spoken down to you or been unkind to you?**

* **Have you ever felt intimidated by anyone?**

* Has anyone ever called you names that still hurt your feelings when you think about it today?

* Is there anyone in your life now who makes you feel bad about yourself? Undervalued? Not good enough?

* Has anyone teased you in a way you found very hurtful, even if you appeared to laugh it off at the time?

We hope that reading the case studies and examples shared in this book will not only help stimulate a memory of a possible cause, but also highlight an event you had not previously thought relevant.

Addressing, challenging and questioning that critical event is paramount. This is achieved by carrying out the five-step process shared in Chapter 2 (see page 38). Your aim is to positively condition your schema by considering positive facts from the originating negative or traumatic event, such as:

* You misunderstood.

* It wasn't personal.

* It wasn't done with malice.

* They behaved that way with everyone.

* It was due to their insecurity.

* They are not in your life any more.

* No one remembers the event, as it wasn't as bad as you had believed at the time.

* You have grown up and changed.

* No one else is judging you for that today. Consider positive reasons why, such as: it felt bad in the moment, but it also ended in that moment.

2 Understand your eating patterns and triggers (ONLY if you overeat)

Our eating habits are often unconscious and spontaneous, and therefore it is important to bring some conscious awareness to how, when and what you eat.

It is difficult to fix or improve something you do not understand, so we recommend keeping a food diary for four weeks.

As well as writing down what you eat and drink, you will need to include as much detail as possible, including:

* **The time of day**

* **Where you are**

* **Who you are with**

* **Your emotion and why you are eating, followed by 'because', for example:**
  * I am hungry *'because'* it's lunchtime and I haven't eaten since breakfast.
  * I am bored *'because'* I have no hobbies, job, don't socialise, etc.
  * I am lonely *'because'* I don't socialise.
  * I am sad *'because'* someone said something/I had an argument/I didn't say what I should have said.
  * I am angry *'because'* of what someone said/did, which I allowed to happen.
  * I feel guilty *'because'* I should be at a family party.
  * I feel bad about myself *'because'* I just don't feel good enough.

Understanding and exploring your emotions will allow you to look for and address the cause of your overeating.

3 Use techniques such as distraction to negate your triggers

Whether you overeat or undereat, your issue is likely a consequence of negative feelings.

While we will share techniques to build your self-esteem and self-confidence later in this chapter, there are many easy distractions that you can use to help naturally elevate your mood and happiness, by creating feel-good hormones such as dopamine and serotonin. These include:

* Dancing to music you love.

* Listening to music you love.

* Recalling happy, fun memories.

* Watching films and TV shows that make you laugh.

* Hugging (and holding that hug for a few seconds).

* Stroking and petting your cat or dog.

* Exercise.

* A walk outside.

* Meditation/mindfulness – which are believed to reduce stress and negative feelings due to the release of alpha waves in the brain.

* Having a massage.

* A healthy diet.

* A good night's sleep.

* Eating foods believed to help create dopamine, such as almonds, bananas, fish, beans, chicken, eggs and avocados.

4 Drink plenty of water

Hydration is paramount to your good health, so be sure to drink water (eight large glasses of water each day is a minimum recommendation). Your brain doesn't function as well when it's dehydrated, so give yourself the best chance of making good choices for your wellbeing by drinking enough.

5 Eat healthily and make sure you get enough sleep

Studies have demonstrated the links between a healthy gut and a healthy mind. Some even call the gut the 'second brain'. You can help your gut by reducing sugar and alcohol intake, and increasing your intake of probiotic food such as kimchi, sauerkraut and kefir, and prebiotic foods such as leeks and onions.

If you feel good, you will gain confidence, therefore it is worth considering how you can promote a healthier way of eating. Perhaps you could consult a nutritionist, your doctor or a fitness instructor, or you could simply start making changes and healthier choices yourself.

However, if you are struggling with a serious eating disorder such as anorexia or bulimia, it is essential that you speak with a health professional who can offer you help, support and counselling to address your issue. We would also recommend researching eating disorder charities for help and guidance.

Being tired or staying up late is more likely to promote eating junk food due to your body needing a quick blast of energy. Prioritise getting to bed at a reasonable time, and winding down at the end of the day.

A healthy body promotes a healthy mind, which promotes confidence.

6 Adopt an exercise routine

Exercise is a great way to get healthy, gain energy and naturally create more feel-good hormones. If you are joining a gym or group fitness class, this is a great opportunity to make new friends and build your confidence.

If you would like more information about eating patterns, emotional eating, yo-yo dieting and tips and techniques to promote a healthier weight and way of eating, you may find our book *Winning at Weight Loss* helpful.

7 Consider confiding in a loved one or health professional

Struggling with an eating disorder by yourself can be isolating, compounding your feelings of loneliness and failure. Telling someone you love or trust about your problem and what you are doing to combat it will offer you support and also make you accountable. Research suggests that we will inherently do more for others than we do for ourselves, so if we confide in someone we respect, we will be more motivated to make progress because we don't want to let them down.

8 Build on your confidence

We have addressed numerous ways throughout the book of building your confidence, which have included practice, rehearsing, imagining, changing your body language, giving and accepting compliments – and practising gratitude daily, which is essential.

9 Practise gratitude

'Cultivate the habit of being grateful for every good thing that comes to you, and to give thanks continuously.'

Ralph Waldo Emerson

It is really important to realise how much you actually have and how much you are capable of. Gratitude allows you to focus on what you do have instead of what you don't.

Conscious gratitude should start from the moment you wake up in the morning, and should include things such as your family, friends, pets, the gadgets that make your life so much easier, such as your phone, kettle, computer and toaster, and the fact that you can laugh and are alive.

You cannot always control what happens on a daily basis and some of the things you might face. However, what you can control is how you begin your day, to help start it from a happier, higher and better perspective.

Something that we have done for many years, and continue to do on a daily basis, is practising gratitude every morning. When the alarm goes off we hit the snooze button (which lasts seven minutes) and we get out of bed. We then sit and during the time it takes for the alarm to go off again we consider everything we are grateful for, which includes: the fact that we woke up, that we can see, that we have our home, a warm bed and our children, and the great things we have done, seen, been a part of and achieved.

Practising gratitude daily will help to put your life and problems into perspective. Also, if you start your day from a higher position, even if things happen that you cannot control during the course of the day that make you sad, your emotions will not drop quite as low, having started from a higher place.

I arrived in a very low place in my life but left in a much better place. My wife has commented many times that I am like a different person.

You two are absolutely amazing and I don't think I will ever be able to thank you enough.

From the bottom of my heart, thank you for everything.

Sam

11

Confidence Within Relationships

Before speaking with you I felt lonely and angry. I now realise my relationships with others were affected by my relationship with myself.

I now have friends. I am my own friend and I am so grateful to you.

Chris

From the moment we are born we begin to form relationships, immediately recognising and feeling soothed by our mother's voice. As we develop, we continue to try to form strong bonds with others.

Relationships are one of the most important aspects of our lives, and many underestimate the value of these connections for our physical and mental health and our confidence. Research shows that those who are more socially connected, whether that is with family, friends or within their community, are not only physically healthier, but also mentally healthier, than those who are less well connected.

We benefit from good, close, positive relationships, as these provide us with comfort, social opportunities, purpose and a sense of belonging, which gives us reassurance and, again, positively impacts our confidence.

Conversely, it has been found that loneliness is a significant contributor to poor mental health, poor physical health and even a reduced lifespan.

It is important to note, however, that the value and benefits of relationships are based on quality, not quantity. Having no relationship is still better than one that is abusive, aggressive, argumentative or toxic. In this chapter we want to share with you the benefits of relationships, and offer tips on how to make, maintain and retain good-quality relationships with confidence within the four most significant categories of life: love, work, social life and family.

Creating Relationships

During childhood, we learn how to engage and interact with others based on the example set by our parents. Just as we copy our parents' accents, we also replicate many of their behaviours and use their social skills as a model when making friends and interacting with others.

It is therefore important to consider the example you were given in childhood when understanding and addressing your approach to relationships. It's also essential to consider your relationship with your parents, which can impact your schemas as to how you address, interact with and respond to others.

For example, if your parents were quite private, introverted or quiet, then you may not have had the opportunity to practise interacting with others and could have copied their behaviours, acquiring the same or similar traits.

Alternatively, if your parents did not allow or encourage you to have an opinion or voice, or perhaps if they were loud or spoke over you and for you, or if they did not encourage you to have friends, then all these situations can prevent you from practising interaction with others, which can go on to influence your confidence.

If you grew up in a volatile home, then you may have created schemas such as 'being quiet is safe' or 'relationships cause anguish' or 'love equals pain' or even 'I'm not good enough, as I couldn't make my parents happy'. The truth is, a child can interpret events in so many different ways, and this can lead to inaccurate interpretations that, if they remain unchallenged, can go on to negatively impact your adulthood.

> **We continue to accept everything that we do not challenge.**

Other people who can impact your attitude and approach to relationships, from childhood through to adulthood, include family members, friends, neighbours, school teachers, work colleagues, partners and siblings. These influences can be positive, helping to cultivate positive relationship schemas and thus confidence in relationships. Alternatively, negative influences can promote negative behavioural schemas, which can be detrimental to your approach and confidence in relationships.

A growing plant is affected by the quality of the soil it grows in, its positioning in or out of the sun, whether it's protected from draughts and the overall care it receives. As human beings we are no different. Our environment leads us towards certain beliefs and behaviours.

The good news is that you have the ability to 'repot' yourself into a better, more nurturing and nourishing environment at any time in your life. With self-awareness and self-care, you can continue to grow, flourish, blossom and bear fruit.

I would like to thank you. You hit a key point with me, which I am sure will have a very positive effect.
Sandy

Draggers, Supporters, Igniters

You will notice how you often adapt in different company. We all behave and feel differently around different people. Some people will bring out the best in you, and you will feel comfortable and confident with them. Others may have a negative effect on you through their actions, and how they speak and behave towards you, making you feel invisible (or wish that you were).

An analogy we often use is cats and fleas. If our cats get fleas, we give them a treatment and within forty-eight hours they are flea-free. While the treatment lasts two months, if they kept away from fleas forever afterwards, then the cats would never need another application. However, as they like going over to the farm near our home to play with the farm cats who have fleas, as soon as the treatment wears off, they get fleas once more and subsequently they need treating again.

The fleas are like the negativity of others. Even if you rid yourself of negativity by working on yourself and building your confidence, if you still surround yourself with negative people who are either determined to put you down or hold you back because they don't like you evolving and making progress, you will find their negativity is catching, just like fleas.

This means that, before you can work on your confidence to make lasting change, it is paramount to consider the people around you and how they affect your confidence. You may want to gain confidence in your relationship, for example, but if your partner constantly pulls you down, whatever work you do on yourself, the likelihood is that your outcome will remain the same unless *their* behaviour changes.

Let's face it, you have a choice as to whether or not someone is in your life. As you build your confidence, you must also consider how other people affect the way you feel. A great process to assess this is to slot people into one of our three categories: supporters, igniters and draggers.

We always say that the best way to work out which category people fit into is by using the mobile-phone test:

Supporters

If they call you, you'll be glad to see their name appear, and you'll nearly always take the call. Supporters are friends and family who do exactly that. They support you no matter what, through good times and bad, through laughter and tears. Whatever you do, right or wrong, they are always there for you and are non-judgemental. You will feel mostly at ease with a supporter.

Igniters

If they call you, no matter what you are doing, even if you are in the shower, you will take their call because they always ignite something inside you and make you feel great. Igniters are rare and precious people to have in your life. When you find one you should hold onto them, as they are wonderful to be around. Igniters are the people who make you feel great and help you to believe in yourself. They are encouraging, and will help push you forward and always want the best for you. You may find you feel more confident around an igniter, who may also have the capability to make you laugh and step out of your comfort zone.

Fuelling your igniters

While doing the mobile-phone test, be sure to add a big sunshine or smiley-face emoji to the people listed in your telephone who are igniters (and perhaps a love heart by your supporters).

If you can, allocate an empowering ringtone to your igniters – for example, the theme from the film *Rocky*. That way, you can ensure that you never miss their calls and that you reciprocate some of their energy by your elevated mood when answering your phone.

Make a point of speaking to igniters and supporters more often, as they are a positive influence on you.

Draggers

When their name appears on your phone screen you will let out a big sigh and question whether you have the energy to take their call. Draggers should be avoided as these are the people who bring you down. They make you feel nervous and uncomfortable, and may contribute to your lack of confidence and self-belief. Draggers may be bossy, bullying, always complaining, angry, constantly negative or lacking in empathy and understanding. They may speak over you, criticise you or humiliate you.

The truth is that most of us do not choose or tolerate draggers in our lives, therefore they are most often family members or work colleagues.

Dealing with draggers

The most effective way to establish the draggers in your life is to do the mobile-phone test.

Look through your list of contacts and imagine how you would feel if your phone was ringing and that person's name appeared on your phone. If you feel reluctance, dread or negativity, then you can safely define this person as a dragger.

Once you have noted who your draggers are, you may want to amend their name and add your own top-secret code by adding a 'D' before their name or a subtle emoji.

If you have a smart phone, to save you even picking up the phone, you could allocate a different ring tone for all your draggers, which will provide you with a 'dragger alert'. Also, if it's a tune that will make you smile, this will ensure the dragger has a more positive effect on you.

You then have three options on how to address the draggers in your life:

1   If at all possible, you need to distance yourself from a dragger as much as you can.

2   If that dragger is someone you are unable to cut out of your life, as perhaps they are family, then you need to change your perception of them and elevate your mood so that when you are in contact with them, even though they will most likely drag you down, you will start from an elevated position. Thus the drop won't be quite so low. This could include adding a fun or funny photo to their profile that will appear on your screen when they call. You may also want to secretly consider them as a TV, film or cartoon character that makes you smile. Or perhaps consider feeling sorry for them that they are so negative; anything to positively change your emotion, but do be cautious. You do not want to hurt their feelings, as it is important to realise that being a dragger is a learned behaviour as a consequence of their own personal life experience, and not intentional.

3   You must accept that you will not change them, as this can be frustrating if you keep trying. However, you can change how you deal with them. For example, if they are sharing doom and gloom, be kind by acknowledging them, but then swiftly change the subject to something that you have been doing, something you have seen or experienced

that is positive. For example, you could say, 'I'm so sorry to hear that, but before I forget I must share with you a great film I saw last week,' or, if they start speaking negatively about someone, you could try, 'Sorry to hear you feel that way, but you'll never guess who I bumped into . . .'

Draggers can enjoy or get benefit from being negative, as most often people will give them attention if they are moaning and complaining about something. It is, therefore, essential to break their pattern. You will have to practise breaking their state and not entertaining their negative talk without being confrontational.

Family

On the whole we are conditioned to believe that 'blood is thicker than water' and that we should be more willing to tolerate, accept and forgive a family member for their behaviours and actions. For many people with a lack of confidence, the following difficulties may arise if you have this belief in keeping the peace with your family, no matter how you feel:

1   You may struggle to speak out to a family member about the way they treat you.

2   You may find it impossible to say no to a family member who places demands and requests on you.

3   You may find it hard to socialise at family functions.

Our elevated tolerance and efforts to please family, coupled with being more accepting of damaging behaviours by them, are at a detriment to ourselves. Furthermore, we are often influenced and socially conditioned to believe that family ties supersede those of friends. As a consequence, family members often feel more able to say what they think or feel, and to air their frustrations and anger, as their fear of loss is often negligible due to this family tie.

The truth is that we are unable to choose our family. Regardless of this, and while this may sound harsh, it is important to appreciate that you **did not** request to be born into your family. You should not tolerate being disrespected by anyone, and this applies to family. You may already be aware of us saying this, but here we go again: you are the only person who will be with you for twenty-four hours of every day, every week and for the rest of your life, and therefore you are responsible for your happiness and deserve to feel happy, and to be treated well and with respect.

CASE STUDY
Aisha: Anger Towards Her Father

Aisha came to see us in our clinic to help her deal with a host of negative emotions, including hatred she felt towards her father. She felt unloved, abandoned, worthless and angry, and did not have the confidence to speak to her father about her feelings. Aisha believed that withholding her emotions was fuelling her anger, and she wanted us to help her overcome this and gain the confidence to tell her father how he had failed her as a child.

Aisha told us that when she was very young, her mum had died, leaving her and four siblings. Her mother had been a full-time mum, caring for her five children, and with Aisha's father at work, she and her siblings had little contact with him.

Aisha said that from the moment her mum died, her world had become a nightmare. She admitted that their home life was chaotic, particularly at bedtime. Her mum would ensure bedtime procedure ran smoothly, but now, every night at 9 p.m., her father would turn off all the electricity in the house and send all the kids to bed without so much as a 'goodnight'.

She had so much anger and resentment towards him because she felt like he didn't care. She perceived his method as callous and loveless.

We asked Aisha, 'Could it be that your dad worked all day, came home tired, fed you all and, when he asked you to go to bed, you all ran riot? Maybe the only way he could get you all to go to bed at once was by cutting the power so you had no choice.' It was evident from Aisha's reaction that she had never considered that perhaps her father was struggling. We further added: 'That may have been the hardest time of day for your dad, too, because he probably missed your mum more than ever then.'

With that one comment, sharing a new perspective, the years of hatred and resentment melted away in front of our eyes. Aisha's reality suddenly changed from resentment to compassion towards her father.

She started to see things from this alternative point of view as she repeated to us that he didn't turn off the electricity to be cruel. She had not considered that he, too, was grieving the loss of his wife.

Once the anger had subsided, the need to scold her father was no longer relevant. However, this did not resolve Aisha's lack of confidence in talking to her father. Their discussions to date had been short and limited to necessities and pleasantries. Aisha admitted she knew very little about her father – or indeed her mother, other than what family members had shared.

We pointed out to Aisha that she did not need to have confidence in talking to her father, as she already had one of the key components. We explained how most people like to talk about themselves, and Aisha wanted her dad to talk about himself and her mum. We pointed out that all she needed to do was ask a question, then just sit back and listen. This instantly took the self-imposed pressure off her, and shattered the nightmare scenario she had manifested in her imagination.

Aisha was amused that this was so simple and could see that she had been a little hard on her dad. We recommended that Aisha rehearse her conversation with her dad, imagining in advance how well it was going to go, and how good and relaxed she felt.

Aisha was so grateful that we had helped her to see that what she had believed was a complicated relationship was a simple misunderstanding, which required just one question to prompt her dad to talk about himself and open up a dialogue.

The feedback a week later from Aisha was that her conversation with her dad had been a big success, and that she realised she loved her poor, now-elderly dad immensely. She was grateful for the opportunity to finally get to know him.

Friends

Friends are like the family we create for ourselves. In childhood they help us to develop our interaction, language and relationship skills, and to create many wonderfully fun childhood memories. In adulthood we find peers with whom we share milestones and life developments.

Having friends gives us people to socialise with, to turn to for impartial advice or support at a time of crisis, to keep us occupied or share hobbies with, to offload our worries to and also to laugh with until our sides ache.

The benefits of friendship are vast, from childhood through to old age. Studies suggest that our close friendships are one of the keys to our happiness in life. Of course, some friendships can come to an emotionally painful conclusion, but there is no sense of obligation or pressure to retain an avenue of contact should the friendship break down. Even if a friendship ends, the fun and memories that you shared should still be recognised and appreciated – recalling these will make the parting less painful.

For some, however, a lack of confidence can impact:

1   Making friends

2   Being honest with a friend about something they have done to upset, hurt or irritate you.

Friendships are often a consequence of chance and rapport. Chance friendships may be made through school, a hobby, other friends, a family member or someone close to where you live. These friendships develop out of proximity and shared experiences and are often effortless – you have been thrown together with these people and a friendship has evolved naturally.

It is less easy to make new friends actively, if your job or family situation makes it harder for you to encounter others through chance and proximity. Finding new friends requires creating opportunities, and we recommend considering the three As:

Acceptance

Accept people for who they are. Do not insist on perfection. We can have numerous friends who can fulfil our different needs. For example, you can have a friend who makes you laugh, a friend who you know can always talk about particular subjects that interest you, a friend who has a similar taste in music and a friend who has had a similar upbringing to you, so you have common views. You are unlikely to find all of this in just one person.

Approval

No one is perfect, but look for something in everyone that you like and approve of. A compliment is a great way to start a conversation, so be sure to point out your area of approval or link it to yourself. For example, 'I really like the way you did that! That's exactly how I like to do it.' Don't be too eager, and don't make a false claim of similarity, as this can be offputting. Give a genuine compliment and it will feel natural.

Appreciation

To appreciate is to be grateful for and to value your friendship or your friend's attributes. Once you have made a friend, be sure to tell them how you appreciate their company. This is important, as we very quickly evolve and take situations and people for granted. As human beings, we like to be liked, so appreciating your friend with a simple 'thank you' now and then will mean a lot to them and make them value you in return.

CASE STUDY
Joyce: Making New Friends

After more than fifty years of marriage, at the age of seventy-five Joyce became a widow and was finding it hard to make new friends who related to her situation. Now that her husband had passed away, despite her friends' invitations for her to join them, Joyce felt uncomfortable, like 'the third wheel'.

Joyce did not want to burden her family to take her out or socialise with her every single weekend, but she was at a loss as to how to make some new friends of her own.

We spoke to Joyce about her hobbies and interests, and things she may have considered but not pursued, and together we collated a list of goals, which Joyce was excited about starting. However, we wanted to ascertain what her criteria for friendship were, as these are an important element of making and attracting friends.

We handed Joyce a piece of paper and a pen, and we also both took a piece of paper so that we could conduct the exercise with her. We asked Joyce to write down a list of everything that was important to her in a friend.

In a matter of minutes, we had completed our list, but Joyce wrote on, and on, and on, and on, until she finally said, 'Done.'

The next part of our task was to count how many points we had each written.

Nik had two requirements of a friend.

Eva had three requirements of a friend.

Joyce had twenty-one requirements of a friend.

Our lists looked like this:

Nik: Honest and truthful

Eva: Fun, kind, honest.

Joyce: Friendly, thoughtful, likes music, wears nice clothes, likes musical theatre, likes to travel, honest, enjoys Indian food, lives close to me, sociable, enjoys a drink or two, preferably a widow, likes animals, intelligent, happy to talk about politics and religion, can drive, stylish, likes bingo, good sense of humour, likes to read.

It was evident to see why Joyce was struggling to find a friend. She was expecting far too much, and of course hadn't met anyone who ticked all these boxes.

As soon as we explained this, Joyce realised that she was being far too picky and understood why her attempts to find friends had so far failed. She hadn't let people in due to her stringent and lengthy list of requirements.

After some discussion, Joyce agreed that the most important attributes of a friend were to be friendly, fun and fair. She left with a long list of goals to give her opportunities to meet new friends, and a short list of criteria of what she needed from a friend.

Joyce's updates were lovely. She soon made some lovely friends at the Toning Tables ladies' gym she had joined, one of whom she later booked to go on holiday with. Her monthly hairdressing treat gave her the opportunity to chat with the staff and regulars, but she also made a friend there to join her at her weekly bingo sessions. She made friends with someone a few doors from where she lived, when she fulfilled her goal of introducing herself to her neighbours who she did not know particularly well.

Friendship Criteria

Take a few moments to write your list of what constitutes a good friend to you.

Once you know what is important to you in a friend, decide which are the top three must-have attributes. Try to keep it to three to give you a wider choice of friends.

> *Friends are the family we design for ourselves.*

Work

It is estimated that we spend approximately one-third of our life at work, and that many full-time employees spend more time with work colleagues than their partners and families.

Work gives us a purpose, financial security, experiences, personal growth, ambition and opportunities. Work also gives us the chance to make friends, perhaps meet a partner or expand our social circles and social activities. On the whole, therefore, work is a positive and incredibly important part of your life.

However, conflict and disharmony at work can make your working day difficult, and even spill into your home life as you long for the working day to end, and then your evening at home is tarnished by the dread of having to return to work the following day because of someone, or some people, and how they make you feel. Studies have shown that a toxic work environment can be damaging to our mental health.

If you are someone who lacks confidence, the chances are you will find conflict at work or challenging colleagues incredibly difficult. You may feel trapped and frustrated, believing that your only option is to bite your lip and say nothing. However, this build-up of pressure can lead to feeling anxious, upset and incredibly sad. Areas of difficulty that may arise at work could include:

1   Conflict with a work colleague.

2   Difficulty interacting with work colleagues.

3   Feeling that you are being taken advantage of.

4   Feeling undervalued.

5 Fear of having to speak in work meetings (see our Sighing Technique in Chapter 7, page 178).

The truth is that you may not like everyone you work with, and that is perfectly acceptable and understandable. However, there are things that you can do to create better relationships, and later in this chapter we will share tips to address conflict.

As work can be such a significant element of your life, it is important to learn to address with confidence areas that cause you unhappiness.

First impressions

First impressions can often be long-lasting. Many studies have shown that first impressions, and how an individual is initially perceived, can influence future behaviour and cooperation. A negative first impression can be hard to amend later.

The good news is that you do not need to have a bucket full of confidence to make a good impression. And you don't need to do anything particularly impressive either. A good first impression can be made by simply walking tall, smiling, making eye contact and giving sincere compliments. A firm handshake and using the person's name in conversation whenever possible helps create a good perception of you.

Mirror and match

As you will recall from Chapter 7 (see page 182), subtly mirroring and matching the person you are engaging with will help to build rapport. Finding commonality is the first thing we usually search for when we first meet someone, in a frantic effort to make a connection and circumvent the possibility of an awkward silence.

Mirroring and matching consists of subtle manoeuvres to adopt similar postures, body language and terminology to the person you are trying to connect with.

Be honest

There is nothing more endearing than a person who is comfortable enough to be honest and vulnerable with others, perhaps by pointing out that they're a little nervous on first meeting someone. Furthermore, acknowledging your nerves can show you care and that you are brave to have addressed your discomfort with them.

It is, however, important to do this in a positive manner so as not to devalue yourself or make anyone feel you are a pushover. So be sure to smile and make light of your nervousness by saying things such as:

'I've been so excited about meeting you, I'm feeling quite giddy and a little nervous.'

'This means so much. If I come across as a little nervous, it is just because I really value you/this job.'

'I do relax, I promise. I just find that first meetings make me a little nervous.'

Listen

Really listening to what people say about themselves, their lives and their hobbies, values and interests gives you vital details to create future conversations.

Remembering the names of your work colleague's partner, children and pets shows you care, and allows you to build connections.

Furthermore, listening can give you the opportunity to offer a random act of kindness to bring you closer. For example, if you hear someone say they love doughnuts, then, if you spot them looking stressed, you could pop out and pick up a doughnut and offer it to them, saying, 'You looked a bit stressed, so here's a little something to cheer you up.'

Ask questions

Most people enjoy talking about themselves, so once you have gathered information from listening, use it to your advantage. Of course, you do not want to appear like a stalker, or as though you are interrogating them with an abundance of questions. Instead, from the intel you collected when you were 'listening', appear interested even if you have to pretend. For example, you could say:

'I heard you mention you go to xyz gym – I'm looking to join a gym and would value your thoughts. Do you think it has better facilities than the other gym down the road?'

'You always look so elegant, do you have a favourite store or designer?'

'You make this look so easy, how did you learn to ....'

Asking for advice is usually perceived as a compliment, as it suggests you respect and appreciate the abilities of the person you have asked.

Create a connection with their good feelings

Another way to build positive connections with work colleagues is by encouraging them to talk about something that created a high level of positive emotions for them.

For example, if they are returning from a holiday, show interest in the destination. Ask if they would recommend it and why. As they relive their happy memories, you will have encouraged a release of positive hormones, and they will unconsciously associate those good feelings with you.

Other examples may be topics such as their son's or daughter's wedding or graduation, the birth of their child or a personal achievement such as running a marathon or earning a qualification. Sharing in other people's happiness will make them feel good, and it will make you feel good, too.

Common interests

A great way to bond with someone is to discuss common interests. You will find, if you are listening to your colleagues, that it is easy to identify the interests you have in common. It may be a television show that you both love, or a sport you both enjoy, or an opinion that you share.

Even if you're not quite as passionate about the topic as they are, showing an interest will make them assume you have something in common, which is important in bonding.

Try to keep the common interest a positive one. We know it can be bonding to talk about colleagues you don't like, or situations that you find difficult, but this negative bonding will not build your confidence or make you happier.

And with colleagues that you see day in, day out, it may be a good idea to avoid topics that could prove controversial, such as religion and politics.

Show you care

Whether it's trying to improve the business for the boss or making life at work a little easier for a colleague, showing you care matters. You don't have to make grand gestures – small actions can demonstrate your thoughts just as well as big ones.

When it comes to your boss, perhaps you could find an area where savings could be made. Present this carefully and tactfully, so rather than saying something like, 'I've found a way to make this better' (which implies that their previous way was flawed), you could suggest: 'I wondered, would doing this help or make savings for the business?'

When it comes to caring for a work colleague, it could be something as simple as offering to make them a cup of tea or to help finish something if they need to pick up their child and are running late.

Team spirit

Joining together with your colleagues for a cause that you all feel passionate about, such as a charity, could help you to break the ice and create unity. This is especially helpful if you have a lack of confidence in striking up conversations with colleagues, as it gives you a reason to be together. And it can help build connections between colleagues who may be experiencing conflict. For example, with your boss's agreement you might organise a company quiz night or lunch-hour quiz, or even paintballing or clay pigeon shooting as a team.

Positive shared experiences build team spirit and foster a sense of unity and connection between colleagues who may otherwise have little in common.

Greetings

Don't underestimate the importance of something as simple as saying a cheery hello each day or going out of your way to say goodbye. It may seem insignificant, but taking the time to greet your colleagues and say farewell is a lovely gesture and shows you care.

Blow your trumpet

If you feel undervalued, be sure to make your boss and work colleagues realise your worth and what you do.

If you have a good idea or have done something to better the working environment, why not send an email about it to your boss or colleagues? You do not need to worry about sounding like you are bragging, as you can make it sound like an update.

For example:

* **You could email your team and say, 'Hey, guys, the staffroom kitchen cupboard was looking a bit messy, so I have cleared it out for us all, but if I have misplaced something or you're struggling to find it, just give me a shout.'**

* **You could go to your boss and say, 'Sorry to trouble you, I've been working on .... today and I just wanted to be sure you agree that it works well, too?'**

Approaching people in a way that benefits them or shows that you value their feedback is a great way to highlight your value to your boss and colleagues without sounding like you're boasting.

The truth is that most people are too busy blowing their own trumpet to notice the achievement of others, so if you want to get noticed at work, you have to dust off your trumpet and make some noise, too.

> *No matter how hard you try to do a nice thing, it will mean the world to some, and yet never be enough for others.*

CASE STUDY
Rob: Confidence at Work

Rob came to see us about an issue at work. He was full of shame and embarrassment.

He had a senior managerial position in a bank where he had been employed for over twenty years, working his way up from cashier to a regional manager and overseeing numerous branches, yet he felt like a fraud. He was being encouraged by his boss to apply for a promotion, yet he did not have the confidence to do so. He was talking in circles as he tried to justify why he needed help, so we asked: 'Are we right in thinking that you're afraid the job will exceed your capabilities? You're worried that your boss will realise this, and you'll be revealed as a fraud?'

Rob was astonished that we seemed to have read his mind. 'That's exactly it. I wonder how the hell I got the job I have, never mind the promotion, and I am literally waiting for the day I make a fool of myself and lose everything.'

We explained to Rob that this was an issue we had come across a lot over the years in our clinic, and it was known as 'imposter syndrome'. Because Rob had started as a cashier, he had underestimated the magnitude of his growth, as it was progressive.

When we asked Rob for his ten outstanding achievements on his questionnaire (as we did with you), he listed only five things:

1 My kids
2 Meeting my wife
3 Being a regional manager
4 Passing my driving test
5 Getting a degree

To start addressing his schemas, we asked Rob: 'When you were interviewed for your promotions over the years, were you interviewed by someone in a higher position? Did you respect them? And were they considered good at their job?'

Rob replied 'yes' to each question.

We went on to question whether he would ever disrespect these senior managers. Would he call them fools or question their abilities?

Rob responded, 'Of course not.'

We asked: 'Knowing that you have been with the company for many years, who do your superiors know best, you or an external applicant?'

Rob responded, 'Me.'

'Who do they have a thorough track record of?'

Rob responded, 'Me.'

'Whose quality of work and ability have they seen firsthand and for many years?'

Rob responded, 'Mine.'

'Knowing that you said they are not fools, you respect them and they are good at their job, who did they choose for the promotions you have had?'

Rob responded, 'Me.'

'And who have they asked to apply for this next promotion?'

Rob responded, 'Me.'

'Who, therefore, is best for the job?'

Rob responded, 'I guess me.'

Rob had never broken down his route to success, nor respected the wisdom of those who chose and backed him every step of the way. The work skills that Rob now took for granted would have seemed impossible to him in the past, and he had lost sight of the experience and expertise he had gained over the years.

We concluded our session by asking questions about Rob's life to subtly encourage him to share his positive achievements, which we added to his questionnaire and top-ten list. When we read Rob's achievements back to him at the end of the session, his list had grown from five items to an incredible thirty-two and included amazing experiences such as skydiving for charity, concerts he had seen, surprises he had given, acts of kindness and more.

We asked Rob, 'Do you deserve that promotion?'

He confidently responded with a smile. 'I'm the best man for the job.'

Love

> *Preventing yourself from experiencing love means you are also depriving your soulmate, who is out there waiting for you.*

Our brains are created to allow us to fall in love, to allow us to feel a plethora of wonderfully warm, enjoyable, comforting and often intoxicating feelings. When we experience falling in love our brain is flooded by neuro-chemicals such as dopamine and oxytocin, and we find ourselves in a state of euphoria.

Interestingly, research has shown that when you fall in love, other areas of the brain, such as the prefrontal cortex, are subdued. As the prefrontal cortex is the part of the brain that helps with making decisions and rationalising, this could explain the origin of the phrase 'love is blind'.

If you have experienced bad relationships in the past, please do not be too harsh on yourself, as a subdued decision-making and rationalising brain could be the reason why it took a little while for you to see the real person they turned out to be.

Evolutionarily, love and bonding are an essential part of maintaining the human race.

Love can offer us security, companionship and someone to share our life and memorable experiences with. However, for some who have endured a painful past experience, their confidence about loving relationships may have been negatively affected. A lack of confidence may hinder them from being able to experience love or to even go on a date.

> **'Never allow someone to be your priority while allowing yourself to be their option.'**
>
> **Mark Twain**

Perfect partner

How do you know when you have met the right person? Often we dream of meeting our perfect match, yet rarely take the time to consider what a perfect match might look like for us. If you haven't thought about this then how do you know what you are looking for?

For example, if you are looking for someone who enjoys classical music and theatre, you are unlikely to find that person at a rock concert or in a nightclub. So if you spend all of your time at rock concerts and nightclubs, you may have your confidence knocked as a result of not finding someone compatible. The fault is not with you, but with where you are looking.

It is for this reason that you should write a list of what your perfect partner would be like. Write down anything that is important to you, including what sorts of things they may enjoy. For example, your list may read: Enjoys going to the gym, likes classical music and theatre. Animal lover, with a full-time job, strong family values, likes to travel and can drive.

Creating a list has a dual benefit:

Benefit 1

You can use your list to guide you to where you are more likely to meet your perfect partner. From our example, this could be the gym, at the theatre, at the zoo or even at an animal charity fundraising event or classical music concert.

Benefit 2

Your list gives you a great range of topics for conversation with potential love interests. From our example above, you might ask: 'Tell me about all the pets you've had', 'What is your usual routine at the gym?' 'If you could travel anywhere in the world, where would you go and why?' 'What's your favourite country you've visited?' 'What concerts have you been to?'

Your list is also a great starting point for online dating, too.

Online dating

If you lack confidence meeting people in real life, online dating is a great place to start as you can list exactly what is important to you and what you are looking for from your list. If you are honest about yourself and your interests, you will attract others who share those interests. The other great benefit of dating online is that you can build your confidence by allowing yourself as long as you need to get to know someone by chatting online first, and then progressing to a telephone conversation before actually meeting up.

Do remember to be cautious when you do finally meet someone in real life, ensuring it is in a public place, and be sure to tell someone where you are going and with whom.

Tell your friends

If you lack confidence with dating, tell friends or family members you trust that you would like to meet someone. Ask them to let you know if they have any friends who they think you would get along with.

If you find going on a one-to-one date difficult then perhaps they could orchestrate a 'chance' meeting at a function or at their home. The chances are that if a potential partner is a friend of your friends, you are likely to get on better and instantly have your friends as a commonality.

Make friends first

Don't put too much pressure on yourself when looking for love. There is no need to view everyone you meet as your future husband or wife. Not only does that put a lot of pressure on you, but it puts a lot of pressure on them. Instead of telling yourself you are looking for a date, just start by looking for a friend, as this is far less intimidating and allows your relationship to develop organically if it feels right.

> *One step out of your comfort zone could be the first step to a brand new life.*

CASE STUDY
Duncan: Dating

Duncan felt uncomfortable admitting that, at the age of twenty-eight, he had never had a girlfriend, which he attributed to his issues with self-confidence.

Duncan described his childhood as uneventful. He had been an only child of older parents, who themselves were rather introverted, rarely venturing beyond the confines of home and work. On discussing this situation a little more, Duncan agreed that his lack of confidence was most likely a learned behaviour. He had not witnessed any particular social interaction from his parents, and as a result he had likely copied their behaviour. He agreed he wasn't 'shy' as he could talk to others – approaching us, for example – but he was unsure of how to make those first connections with a possible partner.

We asked Duncan whether he had met and talked to people during the day at our workshop. He confirmed that he had.

We asked whether he had done anything like our workshop before. He hadn't. We asked whether he had any hobbies outside of his home and work. He confirmed that he did not.

We explained to Duncan that in just one day he had done one new thing, in a new environment, and as a consequence he had met new people. This demonstrated that meeting someone was no more complicated than what he had already effortlessly achieved by coming to our workshop. And a benefit of doing new things was that new friends would enrich his life, and perhaps introduce him to potential partners.

The next element of our workshop was goal-setting and life-planning. We suggested that Duncan add hobbies and joining an online dating site to his life plan so as to meet new people. We also suggested that Duncan write a WOW List (see page 230) and go through our Mirror Technique (see page 220), as shared with you in earlier chapters, to build his confidence and self-esteem. We asked Duncan whether he would be kind enough to drop us an email in the future to update us as to how he was getting on. Here is what we received eight months later:

Dear Nik, Eva and Team Speakman,
Firstly, I'd like to say thank you for such an inspiring day at your workshop. I really did not know what to expect, but I had a truly life-changing day.

You may not remember me, but I came to your Coventry workshop late last year, and I promised I would email you to let you know how I was getting on.

My name is Duncan, and after your workshop I had created goals and promised myself I would sign up to an online dating site, a night school computer course and the gym as a priority. I have now fulfilled these goals, and passed my driving test, too, by the way, and changed jobs, but also I met my partner Alison (we actually started talking at a social gathering with the gym, but chatting to people on the dating site gave me the confidence to speak with Alison).

It has only been a few months, and I'm still living at home with my parents, but so many things have changed in a relatively short space of time, and that is thanks to the boost of motivation I received from you and the fact that you showed me it didn't need to be the huge leap I expected, it was just small steps in a slightly different direction.

Thank you for your help, and I hope to meet you and all the team at another workshop in the future.

Best regards, Duncan T.

Dealing with Conflict

A significant concern that holds us back in saying what we really feel in response to someone being unkind in our relationships is conflict. This may also apply when expressing our disapproval or dissatisfaction about a situation. If you struggle with a lack of confidence, you may shrink from any suggestion of conflict.

Knowing that everything is based on your own individual perception, the first step is to appreciate that you are not in conflict, you are merely making someone aware of a fact. The truth is, the other person may not realise how their actions have upset you. Therefore discussing and not arguing may actually be appreciated.

Your approach should always be calm and open, with words that would extinguish any flames, such as:

'I know you're so kind, so you won't have realised that when you said/did .... that hurt my feelings.'

'It's because I respect you and enjoy working with you that I just needed to let you know that ....'

'It's because I love you that I want to be honest with you and just let you know ....'

'I know you won't have meant it, but when you said/did .... it really hurt my feelings.'

'When you said/did .... I read it as .... I'm sure I misunderstood as you are so lovely/kind, so could you explain that to me?'

Confrontation is created with accusation, blame and finger-pointing, and makes others feel attacked and defensive. It is therefore important not to say, 'YOU made me feel bad.' The trick is to manipulate the situation, so you could say, 'I was a little upset when ....'

To build confidence in dealing with confrontation, take small steps. This could start with asking for a little more milk in your coffee, returning something back to a store or expressing dissatisfaction about a meal in a restaurant.

Practice is also a valuable and helpful tool, therefore imagine the conversation first and rehearse what you are going to say. Follow this by saying the words out loud and then to yourself in a mirror.

Moments before you are actually going to address the person, use our Sighing Technique in Chapter 7 (see page 178).

Saying No

You may feel undervalued and used because you just can't say no and, as a consequence, you agree to do things that are to your own detriment.

Never saying no often leads to people asking for your help more, resulting in you possibly assuming that they think you are a pushover, which decreases your confidence levels further. Conversely, others may assume that you enjoy helping out and to some degree are superhuman as you do so much. If you say nothing and never say no, the end result is often that you feel resentful, while others are oblivious to your dissatisfaction.

The solution is simple. You do not have to say 'no', you can just say 'not right now'.

Next time someone asks you to do something you don't want to do, don't have time for or can't do, your response should be, 'I would love to, but I can't right now.'

'There is little success where there is little laughter.'
Andrew Carnegie

Appendix of Exercises

We hope that you have worked through each exercise in this book systematically. However, for your ease and to allow you to revisit some of our techniques and methods, we have listed them here for you.

Many are forced to resort to courage to get them through a situation or event. However, courage is uncomfortable, causing anxiety, stress and sleepless nights beforehand. Courage is only a temporary solution when you have no other option, and therefore by addressing your schemas as well as working through the exercises we have shared with you, we hope that you can now create everyday, lasting confidence.

> **'The secret of change is to focus all your energy not on fighting the old, but on building the new.'**
> **Socrates**

Conditioning Your Negative Schemas

Your questionnaire and timeline are your sources to locate events and experiences that are the cause or causes of your lack of confidence.

Here are our five steps to help you positively condition and change your low-confidence-causing schema. Working through one event at a time, score each memory for negative emotionality before and after the exercise to ensure that you are feeling better and more positive about each one.

1   Find the original event. Remember that you may have more than one low-confidence-causing event, and that's perfectly normal. Start with the earliest, and concentrate on only one event at a time.

2   Question how you interpreted the event. How old were you, and how did you perceive the event at that age? How did that make you feel? How might that be impacting you today? Consider how your perception back then may have been flawed or inaccurate.

3   See it from an adult's perspective now. Collate contrary evidence to positively condition your perception of the event and your resulting schema. For example, how would you have interpreted it if it were happening to someone else? As an adult, what would you say to that child to make them feel better or to understand the situation from an adult's perspective? What might you say about the other people in that situation? Might they have had issues? Might they have actually not even noticed the effect they were having on you? We share some more examples of considerations to positively condition a negative schema below. However, if you find it difficult to challenge your current belief, ask a friend who you consider wise and positive. Explain that you're trying to improve your feelings by looking for a positive alternative perspective.

4 After working through contra evidence in point 3, through more informed eyes you can now allow yourself a new, more positive perspective so that you can see the event for what it actually was, and not how it felt to the younger you. If you were a third party, and therefore were observing or being told about this event, how might you have seen it differently? Would you have even remembered or judged that person negatively? If not, what emotions might you have felt? Apply those emotions to the younger you in your memory.

5 Decide that you are going to become a victor and no longer be a victim. If things from your past continue to affect you then you are still a victim of that person, experience or event. Make a decision today that you will be a victor of your past: you survived it, you are wiser, more understanding, intuitive and kind as a consequence, and you are ready to free yourself of that past burden.

> *Allowing your past to affect your present is like trying to drive your car forwards while continually looking in the rear-view mirror.*

Challenging your negative schemas and behaviours

Challenging your schemas and offering positive evidence is individual to your own personal circumstances and to each event. However, to help, here are some suggestions of questions you may be able to apply to assist in positively conditioning a past hindering schema.

Was it personal to you?

This is a significant element in our work when helping someone, as often the feeling that you were targeted specifically for being you is detrimental to your confidence and traps you indefinitely as a victim.

It is therefore important to look for evidence as to why it was not personal. For example, we helped a lady who was attacked randomly. When we helped her to realise and she accepted that her attacker had been waiting for a female victim, but not specifically for her, she was freed from this burden.

Similarly, in a violent relationship, although the abuse may feel personal, the fact is that your partner wasn't aggressive only with and specifically because of you – they were aggressive with a partner, any partner and all partners. They will have been aggressive with partners before you, and will be with partners after you, too, because they have aggression issues. This also applies to being bullied. Bullies are not aiming to hurt you personally, but rather to give themselves a sense of power to counteract their own feelings of inadequacy.

Accepting that your trauma was not personal to you negates the belief that you are a target, or that you deserved it in any way.

Are you copying a parent?

If you have a parent who lacks confidence and you have copied their behaviour, then you must consider that you have no reason to lack confidence. The behaviour does not belong to you, it belongs to your parent. Ask yourself: 'Did lacking confidence enhance my parent's life? If not, why not?' When you catch yourself feeling scared and lacking in confidence, remind yourself: 'I am fine – this isn't me, it's my parent, and I am NOT my parent.'

Were you unfairly criticised?

If you were criticised – for example, by a teacher, ex-boss or ex-partner – challenge your belief by asking yourself: 'Do I still want to be listening to that person?' 'What skills did they have that gave them the right to judge me in the first place?' And, 'If they were kind people, they wouldn't have judged me, so I shouldn't be listening to them.'

Are you being held back by a turbulent past?

If there was a time in your life when a series of things went wrong, you may have created an expectation that things will go wrong in the future, causing you to lose confidence in trying, doing, experiencing or experimenting with new things.

Look at the evidence and challenge it. Consider or write down the many things that have gone right in your life. For example, deciding to go somewhere and getting there, passing an exam, making a best friend, having a loving family, buying a home, having children, winning tickets to a concert, baking a cake, cooking a great dinner, getting a bargain on something or going on holiday. If you keep a diary, document one great thing that happened in your day before bed every night. This will start to retrain your thought patterns and create new positive behavioural habits.

Realistically, there will probably be too many things in your life that have gone right to remember, and only a handful of things that have gone wrong.

Rehearsal and Belief

Wherever you lack confidence, see yourself doing the task with confidence in your mind's eye a few times prior to the actual event. Strongly visualise yourself carrying out the task with confidence, with belief and with a smile. This helps you to gain confidence in advance, and will help build your belief in your abilities. Remind yourself, you can and have already done it.

Belief is powerful, and therefore we need you to rehearse to believe in yourself.

Mirror Technique

The Mirror Technique is an effective therapy for you to see yourself through the eyes of love, as you deserve.

You will need a notepad and pen, a voice recorder on your telephone or a trusted friend to help make notes for you.

Stand in front of a full-length mirror. While looking in the mirror, write down everything that you see. Record everything you say when describing yourself; what kind of person do you see in front of you? Are they weak? Are they strong? What do they look like?

Do you see any weaknesses? If so, what are they?

Write down everything you perceive about yourself. Describe the person standing in front of you, both visually and emotionally. How do you feel about that person?

Look at all your body parts, and write down what you see.

Once you have written the list, count how many of those things that you have said about yourself are negative, and how many are positive.

We would now like you to write a list of just the negative things that you have said about yourself.

Look at those words and ask yourself, would you ever say those negative things to a stranger? If not, why not?

The negative things that you have said about yourself, would you ever say them to a friend? If not, why not?

Again, looking at the negative things you have said about yourself, consider whether you would ever say them to your child, partner, parents or a loved one. If not, why not?

Now consider that if you would never say the things you said about yourself to someone you love or to a friend, family member or even a stranger, then we expect this is because it would be mean and unkind. Therefore, please consider that if you are a kind person, and it is not acceptable to say those things to anybody else, then it is absolutely not acceptable to say those things to yourself either.

Now we would like you to look at those negative things you have said about yourself and consider who has said these things to you or who has made you feel this way.

Use the list of confidence saboteurs created on your timeline (see page 22) and explained in Chapter 5 (see page 124), and add anybody else who you feel has contributed to any of the negative, unkind comments that you have said about yourself. Look at that list and ask yourself:

* **Why would you want to listen to that person?**

* **What qualifications did they have to judge you?**

* **Are they even a part of your life? If not, that is possibly because they are not important to you. However, if they are still a part of your life, then consider why they might have said those things to you?**
  * **Is it because they were envious or jealous of you?**
  * **Is it because you have or had something they wanted (e.g. a nice family, nice home, skills, the respect of teachers, qualities they envied, etc.)?**
  * **Is it because they were scared of losing you? Therefore, they thought that by knocking your self-esteem, you would be less likely to leave them and find a new friend/partner, and would appreciate them more.**
  * **Is it because that person felt bad about themselves, and in an effort to elevate themselves they had to knock you down?**

- **Is it because they feared you would steal their limelight? Maybe from a friend, parent, school teacher, boy or girl they were attracted to?**
- **Is it because they were worried that if you became too confident you might leave them or not want them in your life?**
- **Is it because they were worried that you may supersede them in life?**

Once you have considered those things and realised that those words aren't yours but are based upon somebody else or how somebody else has made you feel, what we would now like you to do is see yourself through the eyes of love, so as to recognise your true inner beauty and value, and ignite confidence in yourself.

For the next part of the Mirror Technique use a telephone with a voice-recording option or a tape-recorder as this is the most effective way to do the exercise as it is far more beneficial if you can keep your eyes closed. If not, then keep your eyes closed and write down everything positive that you can remember once you have actually completed the next part of the technique.

Stand in front of the mirror and close your eyes. If you are a little bit unsteady, you may want to get a chair to put to the side of you to give you something to hold onto, or sit on the chair if you are unable to stand.

With your eyes closed, think of someone who loves you unconditionally now or who has in the past. That may be a partner, a parent, a best friend, a colleague, a school teacher, a pet or someone who has even passed away, like a grandparent. Just think of somebody who has or does love you unconditionally.

Still with your eyes closed, imagine that person standing to the side of you. As you picture them standing next to you, shoulder to shoulder, imagine that you are floating out of your body and into that person's body, and looking through their eyes at your reflection in the mirror.

What we would now like you to do – and hopefully you can record this – is to say out loud all the things that person sees or saw in you. So, looking through your loved one's eyes at your reflection in the mirror, say out loud what that person loves about you: what do they see? How do they describe you? Why do they say they love you?

For example:

* **Do they tell you that they love you?**

* **Do they say you are beautiful, kind, intelligent, fun to be around? That you are loyal, that you are perfect, that you are a good cook, a good housekeeper, good at doing something in particular? That you are good at making them feel special or loved?**

* **What do they say about your looks? Do they compliment you on your hair, eyes, figure, stature, dress sense or smile?**

Now, knowing that the person who loves or loved you is not a liar and therefore their feelings towards you are honest and true, say out loud all the compliments that person has ever said about you and everything they love about you while imagining your reflection. Say it as they said it, while imagining that you are looking through your loved one's eyes, and repeat their words four or five times with the love, sincerity and meaning they gifted to you.

Alternatively, use your recording. Press play and, with your eyes closed again, imagine seeing yourself in the mirror through the eyes of your loved one and listen to all the words that person said about you, everything that person loves about you. Listen to the words as you imagine looking at yourself through your loved one's eyes. Repeat this four or five times.

If you can't do this with a voice recording, that is absolutely fine – just remember to say out loud all the compliments and all the things that this person feels, says and has ever thought about you. Keep repeating the kind words with meaning, over and over, four or five times.

Once you have done this and said or heard on your recording all the lovely things that this person has ever said or felt about you, very slowly open your eyes and see yourself for the first time in that mirror through the eyes of love.

See yourself knowing that the person who said all those lovely things about you said them because they were true, and accept that people do not give compliments without reason.

People do not give love without reason. Love is earned, and if anyone has ever or does love you unconditionally, this is because *you* have earned it and because you are lovable.

Now write down all those compliments and positive things that your loved one said about you, felt about you and sees in you. Keep them somewhere prominent. This could be by the side of your bed, on the sun visor in your car, in your desk at work, in your bag or wallet, on the refrigerator door or in all these places. Look at them regularly and whenever you need to remind yourself of how amazing you are, how loved you are and that you deserve to be happy, healthy and confident, reread this list and hear your loved one's voice as you do so.

Finally, return to your timeline, look at your positive list and consider each entry, then consider any positives you might have overlooked or forgotten to add, such as a time when you laughed uncontrollably, a time when you fell in love, whether with a person, place or pet, a time when you were given a compliment or achieved something, a place you visited or a memorable experience, such as a party or a day out. Now you can invest in yourself by reading this list often and reminding yourself of how incredible and fabulous you are, and of all the wonderful things you have seen, experienced, tried or been a part of.

WOW List

The positive list you created during the Mirror Technique, together with the positives on your timeline, can now start to make up your WOW List – a list of everything that is 'wow' and exceptional about you.

Keep your WOW List somewhere you can see it often, such as by the side of your bed, in your bathroom or on the sun visor of your car.

Bungee Technique

This is a great solution to eradicate the negative and destructive emotional connection and impact of the bullies, confidence saboteurs and draggers you have or still encounter in your life.

Imagine the face of somebody you love unconditionally, someone who is a part of your life; this might be your partner, parent, child or a pet. Now, imagine a picture of their face in front of yours (you may prefer to do this with your eyes closed). Just imagine seeing their face and put your hand where you see and feel their image. Most people will notice that it feels as if that picture of their loved one's face is in front of them, very close to their face, maybe slightly to the left or slightly to the right, but it is generally quite close up. Therefore, put your hand where you see or feel the image. Notice where your hand is, and in particular the position.

Try this again, but think about another person you really care about, who you love or who is a part of your life. Close your eyes if you prefer, but imagine their face – again, put your hand where you see or feel it. Again, you will notice that it feels as though their picture is close to you, perhaps in the same place, or slightly to the left or right, or above or below the previous person you tried this with.

Now we would like you to try this with a person you haven't seen for a very long time, somebody who isn't that important to you, maybe somebody you once went to school with, or even an old school teacher – but your feelings towards them are indifferent. You should notice that, this time, this less important person's image is much further away from you and perhaps not as clear.

Having carried out this exercise, it should be clear that your coding positions people who are important to you close to you, whereas those who are less significant in your life are further away.

We would now like to establish your coding of the saboteurs, bullies and draggers you have experienced in your life, and where you see the position of their face. If their actions and words still affect you, your behaviours, your confidence, self-esteem and self-worth, then you may be surprised to notice that you see their image very close to your face. This is based on your unconscious coding. The fact that you have coded them so close to you highlights that their actions have continued to overshadow your daily life.

If you would now like to sever that emotional tie from the past so that they and their actions no longer have any power over you, and you are ready to take control, we would now like you to move their image very far into the distance.

You can do this with your eyes open (or close them if it is easier for you). Imagine this negative person's image, which is likely to be close to you, being attached to a tight bungee cord.

You then need to imagine yourself cutting the cord and releasing them, watching their image fly into the distance, getting smaller and smaller, further and further away until they disappear.

You will repeat this four or five times, seeing yourself cutting that bungee cord and allowing them to fly far into the distance until they disappear.

On the final time you do this, when the image of the person disappears into the distance, close your eyes and sigh three or four times (ensure that those sighs are big sighs), knowing that their image has disappeared and their impact on you has been demolished forever.

Now when you think about the negative person you should notice that their image is difficult to find, far away or you just don't see it at all. You should now have a neutral feeling about them, and you should notice that you feel stronger and more in control.

Increasing self-worth with the Bungee Technique

Just as you imagined people who had wronged you and moved them further away, we now want you to find your image and bring it closer, so you can regain power over yourself and your life with confidence.

Where do you see yourself? Where is your image? You may find this a little more challenging, but look high and low, near and far, or are you even behind you?

Whereas before you cut the bungee cord, this time, with your eyes closed, you are going to use it to pull your picture close to you, near to your face and perhaps even just above your forehead. Imagine that image of you close, clear, strong and confident. Make that picture larger and then sigh three or four times, ensuring they are big sighs.

Sighing Technique

Our super-quick exercise to help alleviate the effects of fearful or anxious events or situations, the Sighing Technique is simple, and can be done anywhere, sitting or standing.

1 Think about whatever it is you are about to do, or your feeling of anxiety and discomfort, and score this out of ten so you know that the negative feeling is reducing.

2 Put your hands together in front of you, interlocking your fingers so they are clasped together (this is not essential but it's better if you can).

3 Now do a large, exaggerated and emotive sigh – this is sigh one.

4 Wait a few seconds, then repeat the sigh and let your shoulders drop down – this is sigh two.

5 Wait a few seconds, then repeat the sigh, allowing yourself to sink into your seat, or relax your body if standing – this is sigh three.

6 Wait a few seconds, then repeat the sigh, this time dropping your clasped hands down to your thighs – this is sigh four.

7 Score how you feel. You should now feel calm or significantly calmer. If not, repeat sighs three and four.

We often sigh when something is over, so thinking about whatever is troubling you and sighing will give you a feeling of achievement and a sense of relief that something challenging is over, and is therefore likely to be another positive benefit of our technique. Ensure your sighs are emotive sighs. Sigh out loud (if possible) and engage your whole body.

Sigh to reduce the negative emotionality of a schema

You can also use our Sighing Technique to address negative memories and events on your questionnaire and timeline.

Picture the event and score your fear or anxiety out of ten. Then, while holding that picture in your mind's eye, carry out the Sighing Technique.

Over-sighing can make you feel lightheaded, so only carry this out in increments of six or seven sighs, while monitoring the score of the negative emotion associated with that memory or event and taking breaks in between.

Keep using the Sighing Technique until thinking about the event gives you no fear or a significantly reduced level of fear.

Pressure-point Technique

This technique offers a great prop and comfort, helping you through social situations or when delivering a speech to a group of people.

Here's what to do:

* **Sit comfortably.**

* **Find the stress-relieving pressure point in your hand (use whichever hand feels comfortable). The point is just below the webbing between your thumb and index finger.**

* **Using the thumb of your other hand, apply gentle pressure.**

* Take slow, deep breaths through your nose and out of your mouth (you can close your eyes if you prefer).

* Apply gentle, firm pressure in a circular motion, thinking about things you have done with confidence and imagining yourself doing your imminent speech or social event confidently (repeat these thoughts, breathing slowly and deeply, with your eyes closed if you can).

* Do this for five or ten minutes, repeating daily.

You have now set up a confidence trigger within your pressure point on your hand. This point can now be used as your prop and support whenever you are out socially, interacting or speaking publicly. It is very subtle and will merely look like you are holding your hands together. Don't forget to keep the point topped up, repeating this quick technique by adding new memories, confident events and tasks you have completed until you no longer need a prop.

Posture

Positively adjusting your posture will positively influence your confidence.

Take a look in a mirror in a seated position, and then again standing. Take a photograph of yourself in both positions or observe how you look and feel. Score this out of ten.

Now we would like you to repeat this exercise, but with improved posture. Lift and roll your shoulders back. Imagine that a piece of string is attached between the ceiling and the upper centre of your chest, lifting you up. Lift your chin, tuck your pelvis under a little and gently bring your abdominal muscles towards your spine. Take a photograph of yourself now, or observe how you look and feel. Score this out of ten.

Your improved posture will positively impact how you feel, and how you feel about yourself.

Practise this adjustment often and it will soon become an effortless habit.

Practise Gratitude

Conscious gratitude should start from the moment you wake up in the morning, and should include things such as your family, friends, pets, the gadgets that make your life so much easier, such as your phone, kettle, computer and toaster, and the fact that you can laugh and are alive.

Practising gratitude daily will help to put your life and problems into perspective. Also, if you start your day from a higher position, even if things happen that you cannot control during the course of the day that make you sad, your emotions will not drop quite as low, having started from a higher place.

> **'Reflect upon your present blessings, of which every man has plenty – not on your past misfortunes, of which all men have some.'**
> **Charles Dickens**

And Finally . . .

We would now like you to revisit Chapter 1, and to add to and reread the positives on your timeline (see page 18).

Look through the scores you gave on the negative items on your timeline. Have they improved? We very much hope they have, but if they haven't yet, the good news is that you now have the tools to make that happen.

Look again at Chapter 3 and your self-esteem questionnaire (see page 46). Has this improved? We very much hope that you are now starting to see and kindly appreciate who you are, your qualities and the fact that you are an incredible person. If not, go back and carry out the Mirror Technique (see page 220) and challenge your schemas from your negative life events.

They were so compassionate, caring and welcoming. It was an overwhelming experience. As a young woman, it's inspiring for me to see two people who are so committed and dedicated to the work they do and it's something I look up to. I look forward to attending another Speakman event in the future.

Melissa

Epilogue

I am writing to tell you about the progress I have made since I attended your Upgrade Your Life workshop (sixteen months ago).

I got up on stage to do the Mirror Technique as I suffered from extremely low self-esteem. Something I had lived with since my youth after being bullied all through school.

I remember standing in front of the mirror and crying at the sight of my reflection, and telling you I felt repulsive, ugly, fat and I never took pictures with my children because I couldn't bear to look at myself.

I desperately wanted to feel more confident as I feared my behaviour would be copied by my kids and I didn't want that.

During the workshop you told everyone to write down a year's plan and a five-year plan. You said not to worry about the how, but just to write it down and that no idea was impossible. Top of my list was to publish a book and I must say, it felt completely impossible then.

December 2019, I submitted the book to a publishing house, half expecting them to write back to me and tell me it was not good at all, but they accepted it. This led me to thinking about what you said in the workshop. 'The more you put yourself out there and get positive results, the more you put yourself out there. There really is nothing that is beyond our reach.'

M.G. Vaciago

We have now shared with you a host of approaches and examples to address your confidence, and we now pass that baton of change on to you.

No matter where you are now, where you have been, what your past looks like, what negativity or traumas you have endured, know that we believe in you. We believe in you because we know you are an achiever. You have proved this by reading this book and showing the determination to make changes to you and your life.

By choosing this book, and choosing to listen to our approach and techniques, you have taken that first step of accepting responsibility for your life from here on in, and for that we applaud and thank you.

Surround yourself with the right people – people who will champion and support you, because that is what you deserve.

Celebrate and appreciate that you have already survived your very worst day, and with the tools we have shared with you, you can now learn to become your own best friend. Take care of yourself, and believe in yourself, as it is you who has brought you successfully to this very day.

Be respectful and loving to yourself, for the world is like a mirror, and therefore if you gift yourself with love, respect and appreciation, the same will be reflected back at you, and in so doing you will become an igniter and will go on to enhance the lives of others.

You already had confidence, albeit perhaps not in every area of your life, and now we want you to cultivate confidence in all areas, to allow it to shine on you, through you and onto others.

Please accept our sincerest and warmest thanks for allowing us to share your journey to everyday confidence. We wish you an abundance of love, happiness and, of course, confidence in every moment of every day of your life.

With love and respect, Nik and Eva xx

References

1   https://www.verywellmind.com/what-is-a-schema-2795873

2   https://www.nhs.uk/conditions/stress-anxiety-depression/
    raising-low-self-esteem/

3   Piaget, J., and Cook, M. T. (1952), *The Origins of Intelligence
    in Children*. (New York, NY: International University Press)

4   https://www.nhs.uk/conditions/stress-anxiety-depression/
    raising-low-self-esteem/

5   Rosenberg, Morris (1965) *Society and the Adolescent Self-
    Image* (Princeton: Princeton University Press)

6   https://fetzer.org/sites/default/files/images/stories/pdf/self
    measures/Self_Measures_for_Self-Esteem_ROSENBERG_
    SELF-ESTEEM.pdf

7   Kim, Eric S., Smith, Jacqui, and Kubzansky, Laura D. (2014),
    'A Prospective Study of the Association Between Dispositional
    Optimism and Incident Heart Failure', *Circulation: Heart
    Failure*. 7: 394–400.

8   https://psychcentral.com/lib/the-power-of-positive-thinking/

9   https://www.mayoclinic.org/healthy-lifestyle/stress-
    management/in-depth/positive-thinking/art-20043950

10 Havron, Naomi et al. (2019), 'The Effect of Older Siblings on
    Language Development as a Function of Age Difference and
    Sex', *Sage Journals*, 30, 9: 1333–1334.

11 https://lancaster.unl.edu/family/parenting/model_537.shtml

12 Quoted from *Pensees* by Joseph Joubert (London: George Allen, 1896)

13 Krishnamurti, Jiddu (1974) *Education and the Significance of Life*. See https://jkrishnamurti.org/content/chapter-2-right-kind-education

14 https://www.youtube.com/watch?v=IAj1xxOJWvE

15 National Institute of Mental Health cited by https://national socialanxietycenter.com/social-anxiety/public-speaking-anxiety/

16 https://socialanxietyinstitute.org/what-is-social-anxiety

17 https://yougov.co.uk/topics/politics/articles-reports/2014/03/20/afraid-heights-not-alone

18 https://www.psychologytoday.com/gb/blog/the-real-story-risk/201211/the-thing-we-fear-more-death

19 https://www.healthline.com/health/alpha-brain-waves#how-to-increase

20 https://brainworksneurotherapy.com/what-are-brainwaves

21 https://news.osu.edu/study--body-posture-affects-confidence-in-your-own-thoughts/

22 Rief, Winfried et al., (2006), 'The Prevalence of Body Dysmorphic Disorder: A Population-based Survey', *Psychol Med*, 36(6): 877–885.

23 Pinkasavage, Emilie, Arigo, Danielle and Schumacher, Leah M. (2015), 'Social Comparison, Negative Body Image, and Disordered Eating Behavior: The Moderating Role of Coping Style', *Eating Behaviors*, 16: 72–7.

24 https://www.nhs.uk/conditions/eating-disorders/

25 Keel, P. K., Forney, K. J. and Kennedy, G., 'Purging Disorder', in Anderson, L. K., Murray, S. B. and Kaye, W. H., eds., *Clinical Handbook of Complex and Atypical Eating Disorders*, 189–204. (Oxford: Oxford University Press, 2017).

Acknowledgements

Our thanks to everyone at Orion for their guidance and support, and for helping us to help others.

About the Authors

Nik and Eva Speakman have studied and worked together since 1992, both sharing a passion to help people lead happier and less inhibited lives. Through studying the work of Ivan Pavlov, John Watson, Jean Piaget and B. F. Skinner, they acquired an intellectual curiosity for behaviourism and conditioning. After many breakthroughs, their studies transformed into the creation of their own behavioural change therapy known as 'Schema Conditioning'.

The Speakmans regularly appear on ITV's *This Morning* and have treated clients from all walks of life, including a number of high-profile clients. They are ambassadors and supporters of Variety, the Children's Charity, and they help many people to overcome a wide range of issues through live workshops, tours, books, radio and TV.

Notes